mustsees
Hong Kong

Victoria Harbour with Two International Finance Centre
© Elwynn/Dreamstime.com

MICHELIN

mustsees **Hong Kong**

Editorial Manager	Jonathan P. Gilbert
Editor	M. Linda Lee
Principle Writer	Andrew Dembinski
Contributing Writers	Florent Bonnefoy; M. Linda Lee
Production Manager	Natasha G. George
Cartography	Peter Wrenn
Photo Editor	Yoshimi Kanazawa
Researcher	Glenn Michael Harper
Proofreader	Anne-Marie Scott
Photo Research	Michelle Bowen
Layout	Michelle Bowen
Interior Design	Chris Bell, cbdesign
Cover Design	Chris Bell, cbdesign, Natasha G. George

Contact Us

Michelin Travel and Lifestyle
One Parkway South
Greenville, SC 29615
USA
www.michelintravel.com
michelin.guides@us.michelin.com

Michelin TravelPartner
Hannay House
39 Clarendon Road
Watford, Herts WD17 1JA
UK
(01923) 205 240
www.ViaMichelin.com
travelpubsales@uk.michelin.com

Special Sales

For information regarding bulk sales, customized
editions and premium sales, please contact
our Customer Service Departments:

USA	1-800-432-6277
UK	(01923) 205 240
Canada	1-800-361-8236

Michelin Apa Publications Ltd

A joint venture between Michelin and Langenscheidt

58 Borough High Street, London SE1 1XF, United Kingdom

No part of this publication may be reproduced in any form
without the prior permission of the publisher.

© 2012 Michelin Apa Publications Ltd
ISBN 978-1-907099-43-4
Printed: August 2011
Printed and bound: Himmer, Germany

Note to the reader:
While every effort is made to ensure that all information printed in this guide is correct and
up-to-date, Michelin Apa Publications Ltd. accepts no liability for any direct, indirect or
consequential losses howsoever caused so far as such can be excluded by law. Admission
prices listed for sights in this guide are for a single adult, unless otherwise specified.

View from Victoria Peak toward Victoria Harbour

Gavin Hellier/age fotostock

Introduction

TABLE OF CONTENTS

★★★ ATTRACTIONS

Unmissable historic, cultural and natural sights

© Alex Havret/Apa Publications

Tai O p 100

© Florent Bonnefoy/Michelin

A-Ma Temple p 88

© Florent Bonnefoy/Michelin

Hong Kong Museum of History p 73

Cheung Chau Island p 98

Hong Kong Tourism Board

© Florent Bonnefoy/Michelin

Tin Hau Temple p 63

MUST KNOW

Mong Kok p 50

HSBC Tower p 60

Wong Tai Sin Temple p 64

STAR ATTRACTIONS

ACTIVITIES

Unmissable activities and entertainment

© Camille Tsang/Dreamstime.com

Enjoy the view from Macau Tower   p 88

© winhorse/iStockphoto.com

Take a cable car to Victoria Peak   p 44

Hong Kong Tourism Board

Have your fortune told   p 50

Hong Kong Tourism Board

Watch a horse race   p 104

© William Perry/Dreamstime.com

Stroll the Tsim Sha Tsui waterfront p 49

© elwynn1130/iStockphoto.com

Discover Senate Square p 83

© Florent Bonnefoy/Michelin

Explore a fortress p 85

© Florent Bonnefoy/Michelin

Taste egg tarts at
Lord Stowe's Bakery p 90

STAR ATTRACTIONS

★★★ ATTRACTIONS

Unmissable historic, cultural and natural sights

For more than 75 years people have used Michelin stars to take the guesswork out of travel. Our star-rating system helps you make the best decision on where to go, what to do, and what to see.

★★★	Unmissable
★★	Worth a trip
★	Worth a detour
No star	Recommended

★★★Three Star

A-Ma Temple *p 88*
Cheung Chau
  Island *p 98*
Chi Lin Nunnery *p 66*
Hong Kong Museum
  of Art *p 72*
Hong Kong Museum
  of History *p 73*
Largo do Senado
  (Senate Square) *p 83*
Macau *p 82*
Macau Center *p 83*
Man Mo Temple *p 62*
Museum of
  Teaware *p 74*
Nathan Road *p 49*
Ruins of St. Paul's
  Church *p 83*
Sheung Wan and
  Mid-Levels *p 42*
St. Dominic's Church
  p 84
Temple Street Night
  Market *p 124*
Tin Hau Temple *p 63*
Victoria Peak *p 44*
Wong Tai Sin Temple
  p 64

★★Two Star

Avenida da Praia
  Grande *p 88*
Avenida da
  Republica *p 88*
Bank of China
  Tower *p 60*
Bird Market *p 124*

Bonham Strand *p 43*
Central *p 38*
Hollywood Road *p 42*
Hong Kong
  Disneyland *p 108*
Hong Kong Heritage
  Museum *p 74*
Hong Kong Park *p 78*
HSBC Tower *p 60*
Jade Market *p 124*
Kun Iam Temple *p 84*
Lou Lim Ieoc
  Garden *p 85*
Mong Kok *p 50*
Seafront Promenade
  p 49
Tsim Sha Tsui *p 48*
Yau Ma Tei *p 50*

★One Star

Aberdeen *p 46*
Avenue of Stars *p 49*
Beach Route *p 47*
Chapel of St. Francis
  Xavier *p 90*
Clear Water Bay *p 54*
Deep Water Bay *p 106*
Dragon's Back *p 102*
Edward Youde
  Aviary *p 78*
Guia Fortress Chapel
  p 85
Hong Kong University
  Museum and Art
  Gallery *p 75*
Hong Kong Zoological
  and Botanical
  Gardens *p 78, 111*

Jockey Club
  Creative Arts
  Center *p 56*
Lamma Island *p 98*
Lantau Island *p 99*
Leal Senado *p 83*
Lo Lo Shing Beach
  p 99
Museum of Macau
  p 85
Mid-Levels Escalators
  p 42
Monte Fortress *p 85*
Ocean Park *p 109*
Peak Tower *p 44*
Po Lin Monastery *p 100*
Repulse Bay *p 106*
Rua da Felicidade *p 88*
Sai Kung Peninsula
  p 54
Saint John's
  Cathedral *p 70*
Sha Tin *p 55*
Silvermine Bay
  Beach *p 107*
Stanley *p 47*
Statue Square *p 42*
St. Augustine
  Square *p 88*
Tai O *p 100*
Taipa Houses
  Museum *p 89*
Ten Thousand
  Buddhas
  Monastery *p 65*

QUINTESSENTIAL HONG KONG

Unmissable activities, entertainment, restaurants and hotels

For every historic and natural sight in Hong Kong and Macau, there are a thousand other ways that you can have fun. *We recommend all of the activities in this guide, but our top picks are highlighted with the Michelin Man logo.*

STAR ATTRACTIONS

IDEAS AND TOURS

Throughout this thematic guide, you will find inspiration for a thousand different ways to explore Hong Kong Island. The following is a selection of ideas to get you started. Sites in **bold** are listed in the Index.

🔭 WALKING TOURS
Central's Skyscrapers

Squeezed between the sea and **Victoria Peak★★★**, the towers of Central reach ever skyward. It's not always easy to walk between the skyscrapers and through the maze of shopping malls, which are connected to each other by raised passageways. The neighborhood deserves a visit, though, for the architectural genius of its looming skyscrapers – **IFC Mall, HSBC Tower★★, Bank of China Tower★★** – and for the last remnants of British colonial architecture, as seen in the **LegCo Building, Saint John's Cathedral★** and **Government House**). Start your walk from the Star Ferry pier, cut through **Statue Square★** and wind up at the **Zoological and Botanical Garden★**.

Statue Square

© Seventhmoon/Dreamstime.com

Chinese Neighborhoods

Dive into the Chinese Hong Kong, just a stone's throw away from Central's skyscrapers and banks. The **Western District** has been inhabited by the British since the beginning of the colony, until they left these lands to the Chinese to flee the plague of malaria that festered here. Old "chop" houses, antique shops and Chinese pharmacies still line the steep streets in this quarter.

The district South of Hollywood Road, better known as **SoHo**, is now the place to go if you want to party just above Lan Kwai Fong, the historical party zone that still attracts tourists and local business people. Contemporary art galleries have opened their doors at the west end of Hollywood Road. Take the Mid-Levels Escalators through Central and the Mid-Levels, and be sure to stop at Hollywood Road to hunt for antiques.

The Waterfront

Best seen at night, the Victoria Harbour waterfront in Kowloon is a favorite setting for tourists and locals who come to enjoy the **Symphony of Lights** laser show, daily at 8pm. Check out the **Avenue of Stars★**, also on the waterfront, which is inspired by the Walk of Fame in Hollywood, California. After the show, head back to **Nathan Road★★★** and walk this "Golden Mile," lined with shops, restaurants and neon lights.

MUST KNOW

KIDS ACTIVITIES
Beaches
What youngster doesn't enjoy a day at the beach? Besides **Deep Water Bay★** and **Repulse Bay★** on Hong Kong Island, and the crowded beaches at Stanley, you'll find some prime sands on the **Outlying Islands**, especially on **Lantau** at **Silvermine Bay★**, on **Cheung Chau**, and on **Lamma Island** at **Lo Lo Shing★**.

Edward Youde Aviary
Amid a wonderland of tall trees, tranquil pools and rushing waterfalls, more than 800 birds inhabit the **Edward Youde Aviary★** in **Hong Kong Park★★**. Kids will love taking the elevated walkways so they can see the colorful specimens from all angles.

Hong Kong Disneyland
Though this park on **Lantau Island★** is smaller in scale than the Disney parks in the US, **Hong Kong Disneyland★★** nonetheless brings the Disney spirit to this part of Asia. No child can resist meeting the beloved Disney characters, watching the parades, and going on the rides here.

Hong Kong Space Museum
Would-be astronauts and astronomers will enjoy this museum and planetarium in Tsim Sha Sui, Kowloon. The daily sky shows in the Space Theatre are always a hit with the whole family.

Ocean Park
On Hong Kong Island, **Ocean Park★** combines an aquarium displaying a dizzying array of marine animals – the jelly fish are

Edward Youde Aviary
© Alex Havret/Apa Publicatoins

magical – with an amusement park featuring harrowing rides like Thrill Mountain. Don't miss the giant pandas, which were given to Hong Kong by the PRC government.

SHOPPING
Shop in Tsim Sha Tsui
It's hard to find such a concentration of luxury goods anywhere else in the world as you'll see in Tsim Sha Tsui, Kowloon. Check out the **Harbour City** shopping and entertainment complex, then browse **Canton Road** for that perfect designer dress or handbag.

Browse Electronic Goods
Even with the competition of online shopping, Hong Kong remains a mecca for electronics. Mong Kok is the place to go to purchase MP3 players, portable devices, and the like, but be sure to compare prices in two or three shops before buying – and always negotiate the price. Even though prices of cameras tend to be the same as in the US or Britain, camera lenses are still cheap in comparison. Plus, you'll always get a package with free items (a complementary battery or memory card).

13

GAMES OF CHANCE
Have Your Fortune Told

Wong Tai Sin Temple★★★, situated in the north part of New Kowloon, is a landmark of the Buddhist scene. Whether you seek luck for games of chance or answers about matters of love, business or life, make a beeline for this temple, which is dedicated to the god of good fortune.

When you arrive in the vicinity of the **Tin Hau Temple★★★** at night, you will come across a host of seers on the temple grounds, who will read the future in the palms of your hands, your birth date, or in the singing of the birds.

Horse Racing

The most popular sport on the island, horse racing holds sway at the **Happy Valley Race Course** on Hong Kong Island, and at the **Sha Tin Race Course** in the New Territories. It's a lively scene on race days – or nights – during the season, which runs from September to June.

BACK TO NATURE
Relax in a Park

On Hong Kong Island, you can take a breather in the **Zoological and Botanical Garden★** or **Hong Kong Park★★**. On **Nathan Road★★★** (in Kowloon), you'll come across the shining white **Jamia Masjid and Islamic Centre** as well as **Kowloon Park**, the "green lung" of Kowloon. In New Kowloon (*beyond Boundary St.*), **Kowloon Walled City Park** offers another escape from the concrete jungle. A former no-man's land, the park now features striking gardens in the Jiangnan style (named for the region around Shanghai).

Take a Swim

After your hike, take a swim at **Big Wave Bay**, **Deep Water Bay★** or **Repulse Bay★** (the first one is a favorite of local surfers). The cleanest water is said to be found in Clear Water Bay in Sai Kung.

Hike a Trail

Easily accessible from Central, the loop trail around **Victoria Peak★★★** is a good way to get some perspective on the territory. Half an hour away by bus from Central, **Dragon's Back★** is an easy hiking trail on Hong Kong Island. Five trails in the **New Territories** begin in Tsuen Wan (*information available from the Hong Kong Tourism Bureau; www. discoverhongkong.com*). Another more difficult trail climbs the Tai Mo Shan (Big Hat Mountain).

Hiking Trail

Hong Kong Tourism Board

THE LOCAL ARTS SCENE
Jockey Club Creative Arts Centre★

This Centre in Shek Kip Mei (New Territories) might be difficult to find, but it is worth the walk. Among the multicolor buildings in the complex, this former factory has been reorganized in to hold galleries and artsy shops, including the flagship of the department story called **G.O.D** (Goods of Desire), a local furniture and clothing brand whose style is inspired by the local culture.

Cattle Depot Art Village

This warren of artists' studios in Yau Ma Tei (New Territories) represents an interesting attempt to enliven the contemporary art scene in Hong Kong. Artists may rent space in the renovated former slaughterhouse, where they create and exhibit their work.

Fringe Club

At night, head for the Fringe Club in Central. This funky building, a former cold-storage warehouse, has been renovated to include two theaters, a bar, exhibition galleries, and a rooftop terrace. Here you can see edgy plays, attend concerts by local musicians, and just hobnob the with cognoscenti of Hong Kong's contemporary art scene.

LOCAL CUISINE

Don't leave Hong Kong without sampling **dim sum**, individual portions of buns, dumplings and more that are wheeled to diners' tables on carts.

And be sure to order a traditional Cantonese dessert after your meal. *Zi ma wu*, or "sesame lake," is a thick soup made from black sesame paste that tastes similar to chocolate. *Keung zap song nai* (ginger milk curd) is made with sweetened hot milk and ginger. Courtesy of a chemical reaction, the ginger gels the milk, yielding a flavorful custard. *Seung pei nai* is a steamed milk custard. Other sweet soups combine beans and coconut milk for a cool summer refresher.

Quick Trips

Stuck for ideas? Try these:

IDEAS AND TOURS

15

CALENDAR OF EVENTS

Listed below is a selection of Hong Kong and Macau's most popular annual events (dates and times vary; check in advance).
For more details check wtih the **Hong Kong Tourism Board: 2508 1234** or www.discoverhongkong.com. For Macau events, contact the **Macau Government Tourism Office:** +853 2833 3000; www.macautourism.gov.mo.

January/February
Chinese New Year
January 1, New Year's Day, is a holiday, but the Chinese New Year (or Spring Festival on the Chinese Lunar Calendar) has far more meaning to the Chinese in Hong Kong and Macau.
A three-day public holiday spills into a week of parades, special events and family reunions. During this time, the Flower Market in Kowloon and temples around the area become hives of activity, and a fireworks display bursts over Victoria Harbour. Gifts of *lai see* (red envelopes containing cash) are handed out to children and those not married, by those who are *(late Jan or early Feb; www.discoverhongkong.com).*

City Festival
This arts festival stages edgy drama, music, mime and other performances. There are exhibitions of local and Asian art too, mainly held at The Fringe Club and City Hall Theatre *(see Performing Arts),* **both in Central (Hong Kong; mid- to late Jan; 2521 7251; www.hkfringeclub.com).**

Hong Kong Marathon
Hong Kong's largest outdoor sporting event attracts some of the top runners from around the globe every year. It involves a full marathon, a half-marathon and a 10K run on courses that take runners from Tsing Ma Bridge to Causeway Bay *(early Feb; 2577 0800; www.hkmarathon.com).*

Hong Kong Arts Festival
Hong Kong's premiere performing-arts event presents an impressive lineup of international and local performances. The festival goes into its 40th year in 2012, with a strong program of concerts, ballet, jazz, opera, and contemporary drama *(various venues in Hong Kong; mid-Feb–late Mar; 2824 2430; www.hk.artsfestival.org).*

March/April
Hong Kong International Film Festival
From award-winning local and international movies to avant-garde indie films, this annual film

January/February: **Chinese New Year**

Hong Kong Tourism Board

16

festival screens hundreds of titles from around the world at various venues. A must-attend for film buffs *(late Mar–early Apr; 2734 9009; www.hkiff.org.hk)*.

Hong Kong Rugby Sevens
This internationally recognized rugby tournament attracts teams and supporters from the world's top rugby nations. Teams compete for four different levels of trophies, and fans from all corners of the globe pack the 40,000-seat Hong Kong Stadium to watch the action on the *last weekend of March (2504 8311; www.hksevens.com)*.

Ching Ming Festival
Ching Ming is a day when families visit and tend to the graves and memorials of the deceased. Grave sites and temples are busier than usual during this festival, with families burning incense and paper offerings in memory their loved ones *(Hong Kong and Macau; first week of Apr; www.dicoverhongkong.com)*.

A-Ma Festival
To honor the anniversary of Macau's most popular deity, the Goddess of Seafarers, the A-Ma Temple is decorated with banners and flags. Worshippers bring offerings, and Chinese theater performances are organized *(Rua de S. Tiago da Barra, Macau; Apr 23; www.macautourism.gov.mo)*.

April/May/June
Le French May
Music, dance, movies, visual arts and some special dining menus – all with a French theme – mark this event, which is jointly sponsored by the Consul General of France in Hong Kong and Macau and the Alliance Française *(various venues in Hong Kong and Macau; mid-Apr–mid Jun; 3752 9978; www.frenchmay.com)*.

Bun Festival
Held annually for a century on the island of Cheung Chau, the Bun Festival takes place around the temple of Pak Tai. Origins date to the early 20C, when a devastating plague on the island abated after offerings of buns stuffed with lotus paste were made to the spirits of the dead. Every spring, three 13m/42.5ft-high bamboo towers are erected outside the temple and covered with sweet buns. Festivities wind up with a procession through the village and a competition to see who can scale the towers to pick the "lucky" buns at the top *(Cheung Chau; late Apr or early May; www.discoverhongkong.com)*.

April/May: Bun Festival

Italy: Quality & Lifestyle
This annual festival honors all things Italian, with a focus on the arts, and, of course, food. The month-long event is organized by the Italian Chamber of Commerce, Hong Kong & Macao *(various venues in Hong Kong and Macau; June–early July; 2521 8873; www.icc.org.hk)*.

Dragon Boat Festival

Tuen Ng in Cantonese, the Dragon Boat Festival takes place on the fifth day of the fifth Lunar month in both Hong Kong and Macau. This fête commemorates the death of a Chinese national hero, Qu Yuan, who drowned himself in the Mi Lo River 2,000 years ago to protest against corrupt rulers.

Today, races with Dragon boats (long wooden caonoe-like boats with dragon heads on their bows) are held in locations around the territory. During the event, it is traditional to eat *zhong*, little packets of sticky rice wrapped in bamboo leaves *(early June; www.discoverhongkong.com or www.sport.gov.mo)*.

Procession of Our Lady of Fatima

To celebrate the Virgin Mary and her miraculous appearance to three children in Fatima, Portugal, in 1917, Macau worshippers dress in white and lead a procession from St. Dominic's Church (in Macau's historic center) to the Penha Chapel for Mass. Along the way, they sing hymns while carrying a statue of the Virgin on a bed of white roses *(Macau center; May 13)*.

Macau Arts Festival

"Enjoy life through art" is the motto of this annual celebration of the arts, put on by the Cultural Affairs Bureau of the Macau government. The festival showcases local, Chinese, and global art forms, with an emphasis on the traditional Chinese repertoire *(various venues in Macau; May; +853 2836 6866; www.icm.gov.mo/fam)*.

July

International Arts Carnival

Organized by the Hong Kong government, the International Arts Carnival is a summer arts festival for families. A mix of performance and workshop programs attract folks of all ages. Often there are shows on ice, featuring marionettes and music *(various venues in Hong Kong; early July–mid-Aug; 2370 1044; www.hkiac.gov.hk)*.

August/September

Festival of the Hungry Ghost

The Chinese believe that hungry ghosts return to earth in the seventh lunar month. During this time, you may see offerings – food, candles and incense sticks – placed on street altars or in residential or commercial buildings to appease the restless spirits *(mid- to late Aug; www.discoverhongkong.com)*.

Mid-Autumn Festival

The fifteenth day of the eighth lunar month marks the harvest festival, which commemorates the 14C Chinese uprising against the rule of the Mongols. Rebels at the time hid their plans for revolt on pieces of paper in round lotus paste- or nut-filled pastries called moon cakes. Today, revelers still eat moon cakes in celebration. Check

September:
Mid-Autumn
Festival

Hong Kong Tourism Board

MUST KNOW

out the lantern displays in Victoria Park in Causeway Bay and Koshan Park in Kowloon *(Hong Kong; mid-Sept; www.discoverhongkong.com)*.

October
National Day Fireworks
Come nightfall on October 1st, fireworks shoot off along Hong Kong's harbor in celebration of China's National Day, the anniversary of the founding of the People's Republic of China. Be sure to come early to stake out your spot along Victoria Harbour *(Oct 1; www.discoverhongkong.com)*.

October: Hong Kong Wine and Dine Festival

Hong Kong Tourism Board

Hong Kong Wine and Dine Festival
A relatively new (2009) event, the Wine and Dine Festival sets up food and drink booths along the West Kowloon Waterfront Promenade in Hong Kong. Related talks and workshops are held at various times throughout the weekend *(Kowloon; late Oct; www.discoverhongkong.com)*.

The Macau International Music Festival
Internationally renowned artists perform opera, orchestral and chamber music, and Chinese folk music, in a symphonic blend of East and West. Various venues include several World Heritage Sites, including the Dom Pedro V Theatre, Mount Fortress and St. Dominic's Church *(Macau; Oct-early Nov; +853 2836 6866; www.icm.gov.mo/fimm)*.

November/December
Macau Grand Prix
Probably the most internationally known event held in Macau, the Grand Prix has been going strong here for more than 50 years. Both car and motorcycle races follow a 6.2km/3.8mi city circuit; grandstands are set up along the route *(mid-Nov; +853 8796 2268; www.macau.grandprix.gov.mo)*.

Macau Food Festival
A favorite among locals and visitors, the Macau Food Festival is organized by the Association of Macau Restaurant Merchants. More than 100 booths showcase Asian, European, Mainland China and local delicacies *(mid-to late Nov; +853 2857 5765; www.macautourism.gov.mo)*.

Macau International Marathon
This international marathon, first held in Macau in 1981, continues to attract large numbers of international long-distance runners. Both a full and a half-marathon traverse the territory *(early Dec; www.macaumarathon.com)*.

Christmas Celebrations
During Christmas and on Boxing Day, Hong Kong's skyscrapers form the backdrop for giant illuminations with festive flavor. On New Year's Eve, join the crowds at Times Square in Causeway Bay or in Lan Kwai Fong in Central to count down the *New Year (Dec 31)*.

CALENDAR OF EVENTS

PRACTICAL INFORMATION

WHEN TO GO

A subtropical climate in Hong Kong, which shares a latitude close to Hawaii's, means that the weather is warm to hot for most of the year. The majority of visitors come during the more moderate – and sometimes rainy – spring months of March to May, when T-shirts and shorts are often appropriate. The driest period is from late September until the end of November, Hong Kong's short autumn. Winters can be cold, dipping to 6°C/4°F at night. Summer temperatures, on the other hand, rise to 35°C/95°F at times, with humidity building up to heavy downpours that clear the muggy air.

Typhoons usually strike a few times a year, typically from June to October; this only rarely calls for concern if the signal reaches 8 or above, when land, sea and air transport usually stops.

The best clothes to wear in Hong Kong's warm, humid climate are cottons or modern climate-control fabrics. An umbrella is always useful; it can double as a parasol, a popular use among Hong Kongers. Be sure to carry a bottle of drinking water in order to stay hydrated. Visitors unaccustomed to the more humid seasons may find themselves quickly tired; plan to take breaks during the day.

KNOW BEFORE YOU GO
Useful Websites
www.hk.asia-city.com
HK magazine's online listings are a good source of what's doing in Hong Kong on stage, screen and in galleries.

www.openrice.com
A no-nonsense restaurant review site for every class of eatery, from noodle shops upwards; select by food type or neighborhood.

www.womguide.com
The WOM, short for Word of Mouth, guide offers short food reviews plus longer foodie features, written by chefs as well as other food-minded types.

Tourism Offices and Information Centers
www.discoverhongkong.com
Contact the Hong Kong Tourism Board prior to arriving.

www.hko.gov.hk
Check online with the Hong Kong Observatory for 5-day weather forecasts and typhoon warnings.

Hong Kong International Airport Visitor Centre –
Buffer Halls A and B, Arrivals Level, Terminal 1.

Hong Kong Island Visitor Centre – The Peak Piazza, between The Peak Tower and The Peak Galleria.

Kowloon Visitor Centre – Star Ferry Concourse, Tsim Sha Tsui.

Average Seasonal Temperatures in Hong Kong				
	Jan	**Apr**	**Jul**	**Oct**
Avg. High	15°C/59°F	27°C/81°F	33°C/91°F	29°C/84°F
Avg. Low	8°C/46°F	18°C/64°F	26°C/79°F	21°C/70°F

International Visitors

China Embassies in North America

Hong Kong, being a Special Administrative Region (SAR) of China, falls under Chinese Embassies, which are found across Europe, North America and Asia. Consulates have both Hong Kong and Macau under their jurisdiction.

◆ Canada

Ottawa: 515 St. Patrick Street, Ottawa, Ontario K1N 5H3; *+1-613-789-3434; ca.china-embassy.org.*
Toronto: 240 George Street; Toronto Ontario M5R 2N5; *+1-416-964-9646 or +1-403-264-3322; toronto.china-consulate.org.*
Vancouver: 3380 Granville Street, Vancouver, British Columbia V6H 3K3; *+1-604-734-7492 or +1-604-7340704; vancouver. chineseconsulate.org/eng.*

◆ USA

New York: 520 12th Ave., New York, NY 10036; *+1-212-244-9456.*
Los Angeles: 443 Shatto Place, Suite 300, Los Angeles, CA 90020; *+1-213-807-8088.*
Washington, DC: 2201 Wisconsin Ave. NW, Room 110, Washington, DC 20007; *+1-202-338-6688 or + 1-202-588-9760.*

Central District
Hong Kong Tourism Board

Foreign Embassies in Hong Kong

British Consulate: 1 Supreme Court Road, Admiralty; *2901 3000; www.britishconsulate.org.hk.*
Canada: 12th-14th Floor, Tower 1, Exchange Square, 8 Connaught Place, Central; *3719 4700; www.hongkong.gc.ca.*
USA: Consulate-General, 26 Garden Road, Central; *2523 9011; hongkong.usconsulate.gov.*

Entry Requirements

Most visitors just need a valid passport to enter Hong Kong. UK passport holders are allowed to stay for six months; nationals of other EU countries, Australia, Canada, New Zealand, the US and some other countries can stay three months.
Those who wish to stay longer, must apply for a visa before (ideally six weeks in advance) traveling to Hong Kong.
Hong Kong Immigration website: www.immd.gov.hk.

Hong Kong Customs

Visitors over 18 can import most things for personal use (including an unlimited amount of cash), but note that recent **tobacco laws** allow only 19 cigarettes (or 1 cigar or 25 grams of small cigars / 25g of tobacco) and one liter of **spirits**. (Wine and other alcoholic beverages below 30% alcohol by volume are unrestricted.) For details, *see www.customs.gov.hk.*

Health

No vaccinations are required to enter Hong Kong. Some doctors recommend immunization against flu and tetanus. Air pollution is relatively high; those with serious

PRACTICAL INFORMATION

21

respiratory conditions should take appropriate medications.

Ambulance – Dial 999 for an ambulance

Health Services – Many hotels have a doctor on-call 24hrs. There are several international health services available to tourists. Hong Kong's government health-care system charges visitors HK$570 to use Accident & Emergency services at public hospitals and clinics. The largest **government hospitals** are:
Queen Elizabeth Hospital, 30 Gascoigne Road, Kowloon; *2958 8888*.
Queen Mary Hospital, 102 Pok Fu Lam Road, Hong Kong Island; *2855 3838*.
Traditional Chinese treatments, such as acupuncture and herbal medicine, are offered at several public hospitals. A list of licensed practitioners is available from the Chinese Medicine Council of Hong Kong *(www.cmchk.org.hk)*.

Hospital Authority help-line: *2300 6555; www.ha.org.hk.*

Private 24-hour doctor and outpatient services:
Hong Kong Central Hospital – 1B Lower Albert Road, Central; *2522 3141*.

Hong Kong Adventist Hospital – 40 Stubbs Road, Mid-Levels, Hong Kong Island; *3651 8888; www.hkah.org.hk.*
Hong Kong Baptist Hospital – 222 Waterloo Road, Kowloon Tong, Kowloon; *2339 8888.*

Pharmacies – Two healthcare and pharmacy companies, **Watsons** *(www.watsons.com.hk)* and **Mannings** *(www.mannings.com.hk)* are found across Hong Kong. Independent pharmacies (identified by a red cross) also abound, as do traditional Chinese herbalists. Pharmacies generally only accept prescriptions issued by a doctor in Hong Kong.

Etiquette and Language
Hong Kong's dress code used to be more formal than in the West but is now relaxing a little; businessmen and women do not have to be quite so formally attired. In upscale bars and restaurants, there is often a no-jeans-or-sneakers rule in effect. In lower-priced restaurants, and in people's homes, table etiquette encourages guests to pick up a personal rice or noodles bowl, in order to catch ingredients while eating, rather than allowing them to drop on the table. Casual dining also allows the placing of gristle and bone fragments onto the plastic table

Bilingual Is Best
Keep the business card of your hotel with its name written in Chinese. You'll find this may come in handy to show your taxi driver, so he'll know where to take you. Chinese-language addresses or place names are also useful, so consider asking the staff at your hotel to write this down for you before you leave. If you'd like to try to say your destination in Chinese, also ask a concierge or other helpful staff member to pronounce it a few times; then write down what you hear in phonetic form.

Hong Kong International Airport

tops, which are later wiped clean. Official signage in Hong Kong is in Chinese and English; in smaller businesses and restaurants, the language used is often Chinese. Cantonese is Hong Kong's first language and conversation in it is often quite animated and delivered at higher volume than some other languages. In English, the second language in Hong Kong, you may receive some very direct observational remarks; this results from a direct translation from Cantonese, a no-nonsense Chinese dialect. That said, people can be quite guarded about discussing money and personal matters with those they do not know well. Mandarin, the first language of Mainland China, is increasingly spoken in Hong Kong.

GETTING THERE
By Air

Even though Hong Kong was transferred to China in 1997, when arriving from Mainland China (meaning the People's Republic of China, excluding Hong Kong and Macao), Hong Kong is considered an international destination. It is often less expensive to fly to nearby Shenzhen. From that airport, you can take a shuttle bus to Hong Kong.

Hong Kong International Airport is located on the artificially leveled island of Chek Lap Kok, in the north of Lantau Island *(Outlying Islands; 2181 8888; www.hongkongairport.com)*. Regarded by many to be the best airport hub in Asia, this airy and efficient airport was designed by British architect Norman Foster. From here, it takes less than 30 minutes to reach downtown via Airport Express. The airport has two main terminals, with Terminal 1 home to local carrier Cathay Pacific; other major and smaller airlines share the two terminals.

Airport Tax – A passenger departure tax of HK\$120 per person (12 years and above) is built into the airline ticket price.

Airlines Using Chek Lap Kok:
◆ **Cathay Pacific**
Suite1808, 18th floor, The Gateway, 9 Canton Road, Harbour City, Tower 6, Tsim Sha Tsui, Kowloon; *2747 1888; www.cathaypacific.com.*
◆ **Air France**
8th floor, 199 Des Voeux Road Central, Vicwood Plaza, Sheung Wan, Hong Kong Island; *2501 9498; www.airfrance.com.*
◆ **Lufthansa**
Unit 2001-4, 20th floor, The Broadway, 54-62 Lockhart Road, Wan Chai, Hong Kong Island; *2868 2313; www.lufthansa.com.*
◆ **Air China**
2nd floor, CNAC Building, 10 Queen's Road, Central, Hong Kong Island; *3102 3030; www.airchina.cn.*
◆ **China Southern Airlines**
18th floor, United Centre, 95 Queensway, Admiralty, Hong Kong Island; *2929 5033; www.csair.com.*
Lost baggage – Terminal 1, level 6; *2182 2018.*

PRACTICAL INFORMATION

Airport Tipping – Tipping is not appropriate at the airport.

Taxi – Metered taxis wait outside the terminals. Red taxis serve destinations throughout Hong Kong, while green taxis cover the New Territories. Blue taxis go to Lantau Island. By taxi, it will cost around HK$300 to reach Tsim Sha Tsui (Kowloon) and HK$350 to Central and Causeway Bay (Hong Kong Island). The price can rise rapidly if you run into traffic jams.

Airport Express – This rail line, part of and linked to the MTR system, is the quickest way downtown, reaching Hong Kong station (*HK$100, one way; HK$189, round-trip*) in 24 minutes, and Kowloon (*HK$90, one way; HK$160, round-trip*) in 21. First and last trains run in both directions daily, at 5:50am and12:48am.
Free shuttle buses run between Central and Kowloon Airport Express stations to many hotels. Passengers can check in bags at Airport Express stations, up to an evening before departure.
Check all details at *www.mtr.com. hk/eng/airport_express*.

Airport Buses – Buses run to most corners of the territory, day and night *(see www.hongkongairport. com for routes and timetables)*.

By Boat/Ferry

Cruise ships dock at the Ocean Terminal in Tsim Sha Tsui, right next to the Star Ferry terminal. If arriving from Mainland China or Macau by ferry, passengers arrive either at the China Ferry Terminal in Tsim Sha Tsui, Kowloon, or at the Shun Tak Centre in Sheung Wan, Hong Kong Island.

By Train

If you arrive by train in Shenzhen, you just need to cross the border on foot at Lowu, where the Kowloon-Canton Railway (KCR) takes you directly to Kowloon and links up with the Hong-Kongwide MTR train system (*48min to Tsim Sha Tsui East; HK$36.50*).

Mainland "Through Trains"
Hung Hom Station – *8 Cheong Wan Road, Kowloon; 2947 7888*. Through trains for Mainland China arrive and depart from this station. Buy tickets directly at the station, on its website for some Southern China Destinations *(www.it3.mtr. com.hk)*, or in one of the many China Travel Service (CTS) agencies in the city (*opposite*). The Hong Kong-Guangzhou express train shuttles back and forth 12 times per day between 7:25am and 7:24pm (*2hrs; approx. HK$200*). Some trains stop at Dongguan. Direct line to Shanghai (*18.5hrs; HK$508, one-way, for sleeper berth*), and to Beijing (*West Railway Station; 23.5hrs; starting at HK$574 for sleeper*).

Shenzhen Lowu Station – *Jianshe Lu*. Express trains between Shenzhen and Guangzhou (East station) depart every 5–10min from 6:20am–10:40pm (*just over 1hr; RMB75*). Buy ticket at station up to 15 minutes before departure. Trains depart between Shenzhen and Guilin from here too (*13hrs; RMB300 for a basic sleeper*).

China Travel Service (CTS) – A good one-stop travel agent for tickets and visas for Mainland China

Florent Bonnefoy/Michelin

Macau Ferry Terminal – 202 Connaught Road Central, Sheung Wan, Hong Kong Island. 24-hour departure for Macau with TurboJet (*1hr; HK$150*) and Chu Kong Passenger Transportation Co. *(Taipa jetty; every 30min from 7am – 1am; 1hr 15min; HK$135).* Departure for Shenzhen *(Shekou jetty; 1hr; HK$125)* and for Guangzhou *(Lianhuashan jetty; 2hrs; HK$165).*

visits *(www.ctshk.com)*. There are **three locations in Hong Kong**: **2-20 Paterson St.**, Hang Lung Centre, Room 606, 6th floor, Causeway Bay, Hong Kong Island, *2808 1131*.
33 Canton Road, China HK City Office, Shop 14A, Tsim Sha Tsui, Kowloon, *2736 1863*.
636 Nathan Road, Bank Centre, Room 312, 3rd floor, Mong Kok, Kowloon, *2388 8607*.

By Bus
CTS buses run to several cities in Southern China (Guangdong). This is inexpensive, if you have the time. For Guangzhou, departures leave from all over the city from 6:50am –10:15pm *(consult www.ctshk.com).* Starting points include the Metro Park Hotel in Causeway Bay, Wan Chai ferry pier, the Hung Hom Coliseum (next to the train station), and in front of CTS agencies in Sheung Wan, on Hong Kong Island and in Prince Edward, Kowloon.

By Boat
You can take the ferry from Hong Kong to several cities in Guangdong. Boats arrive at Macau Ferry Terminal (Hong Kong Island), China Ferry Terminal (Kowloon) or the Sky Pier (airport).

China Ferry Terminal – 33 Canton Road, Kowloon. Ferries depart for Macau from 7am– 10:30pm with **New World First Ferry** (*1 hr 15 min; HK$150*). Departures for Canton at 7:50am, 10:40am, 1:50pm and 6:10pm with **Chu Kong Passenger Transportation Co**. *(Lianhuashan jetty; 2 hrs; HK$170).* Ferries for Shenzhen *(Shekou jetty; 1 hr; RMB110)* and for the Fuyong jetty *(next to Shenzhen Airport; departs Mon–Fri 8:45am, and 4:30pm in the other direction; 1hr; RMB190).*

Sky Pier – Travelers using the Sky Pier at Hong Kong International Airport – including international passengers and PRD residents – are not required to go through immigration and customs at Hong Kong International Airport, making air-to-sea or sea-to-air transfers hassle-free.
 Eight port connections in the PRD and Macau include Zhongshan, Zhuhai Jiuzhou, Dongguan Humen, Guangzhou Nansha, Shenzhen Shekou and Shenzhen Fuyong, as well as Taipa and Maritime Ferry Terminal in Macau.
Departures for Shenzhen are approximately every hour from 9am to 9:20pm with Chu Kong

Passenger Transportation Co.
(to Shekou jetty; 30min; HK$220).

Ferry Companies
◆ **TurboJet**
2859 3333; www.turbojet.com.hk.
You can also buy your advance
TurboJet tickets from any CTS
branch.
◆ **Chu Kong Passenger**
Transportation Co.
2858 3876; www.cksp.com.hk.
◆ **New World First Ferry**
2131 8181; www.nwff.com.hk.

GETTING AROUND
Octopus Cards
Save time and money on fares
with stored-value Octopus travel
cards. Each costs a refundable
HK$50 and can be renewed at MTR
stations, some ferry ticket booths
and convenience stores (7-Eleven;

Wellcome Supermarket). Some fast-
food restaurants accept payment
with the card.

Discounts
Travelers over 65 and children
under 11 travel half-fare on most
transport; children under three
travel free.

Mass Transit Railway (MTR)
The MTR is an exemplary
underground rail network in
the city, which is becoming
more above-ground in the New
Territories. This fast, clean and
reasonably priced network runs
from around 6am–12:30am.
Automatic machines dispense
tickets or recharge Octopus cards
at all stations. Everything is posted
in English and Chinese, and on-

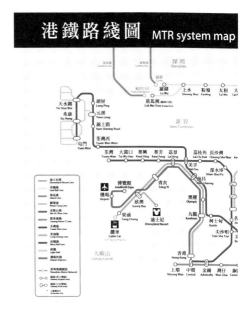

港鐵路綫圖　MTR system map

train stop announcements are multi-lingual. Stations have well-marked exits, identified by letters and numbers; there are good local area maps at all stations. Much of the city is covered, right up to the Lowu border with Shenzhen, PRC. **Blue line (Island line)** departs from Sheung Wan for Chai Wan and serves Central, Wan Chai, Causeway Bay and North Point.

Red line (Tsuen Wan Line) goes up through the north of Hong Kong and passes through Tsim Sha Tsui, Jordan and Mong Kok en route to the New Territories.

Yellow line (Tung Chung Line) runs from Hong Kong Island to Lantau.

Departing from Yau Ma Tei, the **Green line (Kwun Tong Line)** serves Mong Kok, Shek Kip Mei, Wong Tai Sin and the western area.

Light-blue line (East Rail Line) connects Lo Wu (Shenzhen) and Tsim Sha Tsui East. Main stops: Tai Po, Sha Tin, and Hung Hom station. **Brown line (Ma On Shan Line)** serves the eastern side of the area. **Purple line (Tseung Kwan O Line)** connects Hong Kong Island (North Point) with Po Lam (east). **Light-purple line (West Rail Line)** runs to the New Territories, and Yuen Long. Two special lines transport passengers to the airport and to Hong Kong Disneyland. New lines are due to open in the next few years. Information: *2881 8888; www.mtr.com.hk*.

By Bus
A comfortable means of public transportation, buses crisscross the city at frequent intervals, especially during rush hour.

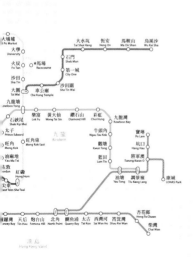

PRACTICAL INFORMATION

Buses are a good way to get to the south of Hong Kong Island, but the network is complex, a result of the MTR serving all the principle destinations. If you are paying in cash, have the exact amount ready or use a stored-value Octopus card. Most buses run 6am–midnight, but there are also overnight routes. Drivers rarely speak much English, but dual digital and audio announcements on most announce stops in English and Chinese. Pick up free bus routes maps at HKTB information centers.

Minibuses also cover most neighborhoods; although faster than large buses, these require guidance, as timetables are Chinese-only and bus stops are unannounced.

By Taxi

Taxis are easy to hail on the street, except during rush hours or when it rains. There are three colors: red on Hong Kong Island and Kowloon; green in the New Territories, and blue on Lantau. Starting fare for red cabs is HK$18, with additional charges for luggage placed in the trunk, advance telephone booking, and tunnel and bridge tolls. All fares are metered, and receipts are available. By law, passengers in front or back seats must wear seat belts. *Call a cab: 2571 2929.*

By Car

It is easy to rent a car in Hong Kong and this is a good way of exploring the New Territories. An international drivers license is all that is needed. Rates are a little higher than in some other places, starting at HK$800-900 per day, with discounts for longer periods. A notable exception is Hawk Rent

A Car. In the urban areas, heavy traffic and expensive parking fees, combined with the availability of low-priced taxis and public transport, make driving pointless.

Car Rental Companies

Avis – Hopewell Centre, 17th flr., 183 Queen's Road East, Wan Chai, Hong Kong Island; *2882 2927.* **67 Mody Road**, Shop 46, basement level, Peninsula Centre, Tsim Sha Tsui East, Kowloon; *2890 6988. www.avis.com.hk.*
Hawk Rent A Car – Rentals are delivered to a specified location. *2516 9822. www.hawk rentacar.com.*

Rules of the Road

Keep the following in mind:

- Foreign or international **driving licenses** may be used for most car-rental firms.
- Drive on the **left-hand side** of the road.
- **Speed limit:** 50kph/31mph on secondary roads, and up to 110kph/68mph on highways.
- **Seat belts** are mandatory in front and back seats. Child safety seats are not compulsory.
- Use **headlights** at night.
- Do not drink and drive.

By Bicycle

Urban Hong Kong is not cycle-friendly, and few peddlers brave the dense traffic and exhaust fumes. Bike trails, however, do exist in and around the Tai Po area of the New Territories.
The most scenic trail skirts the Plover Cove Reservoir. Tai Po town itself and alongside the waterfront of a connecting highway between Tai Po and Sha Tin also have trails that attract bicyclists.

MUST KNOW

Hong Kong Tourism Board

Bicycle Rentals

- **Tai Po**
  Several shops outside Tai Po Market KCR station rent bicycles from around HK$60 per day.
- **Outlying Islands**
  Friendly Bicycle Shop, Shop 12, Mui Wo Centre, Mui Wo, Lantau Island; *2984 2278*. In Silvermine Bay, near the ferry jetty, this shop rents bikes out for HK$150 per day. Cheung Chau and Lamma Island (Yung Shue Wan) also have bike-rental shops.

By Tram

Skirting Hong Kong Island's north shore is a collection of century-old clunking cast-iron trams.
The exact flat fare is a bargain at HK$2 for adults; pay as you exit *(Hong Kong Tramways: 2548 7102; www.hktramways.com)*.
The so-called **Peak Tram** is actually a funicular railway, hauled up from the Admiralty city terminus to the one within the Peak Tower *(20min; 2522 0922; www.the peak.com.hk; see Regions/Hong Kong Island North)*.

By Ferry

Star Ferries

Like its tram cousins, this is arguably more of a Hong Kong icon than an efficient form of transport. Nevertheless, a trip across ever-diminishing Victoria Harbour on the green and white open-sided ferries is a must-do. The trip takes 10 minutes between Central and Tsim Sha Tsui.

The Star Ferry runs daily 6:30am–11:30pm, at intervals of less than 10 minutes *(HK$2.50 for upper deck; HK$2 for lower deck)*. A service also runs between Wan Chai and Tsim Sha Tsui Line departing every 8 to 20 minutes, depending on time and day *(Mon–Fri, 7:10am–11pm; Sat, Sun and holidays every 12-29min from 7:30am–1pm; HK$2.50 weekdays, HK$3 weekends)*.
Star Ferry information line: *2367 7065; www.starferry.com.hk*.

Outlying Island Ferries

Ferries to Cheung Chau, Lamma, Lantau, and Peng Chau leave from Outlying Ferry Piers 1–6 in Central, and next to the Star Ferry Piers in Central on Hong Kong Island *(all take 30min–1hr each way)*. Two types of boats cover these routes: the standard ferries and the slightly more expensive fast ferries.
New World First Ferry Services Ltd. provide service to Cheung Chau, Peng Cahu and Mui Wo on Lantau Island *(2131 8181; www.nwff.com.hk)*.
The **Hong Kong & Kowloon Ferry** runs to Lamma Island *(2815 6063; www.hkkf.com.hk)*. Check websites for fees and time tables.

BASIC INFORMATION
Accessibility

Hong Kong, frankly, is not the easiest destination for travelers with disabilities to navigate. Access is tailored for the disabled at the airport, large hotels and some new shopping malls and office buildings. The MTR does have ramps and lifts in all stations, but they take time to locate; buses do not have entrance panels that can be lowered. Taxis are the easiest way to travel. Access information to public buildings and attractions is listed at HKTB information centers and on its website: *www.discoverhongkong.com*. For access at public transport facilities, check the Transport Department website: *www.td.gov.hk*.

Accommodations

For suggested lodgings, see Hotels.

The Hong Kong Tourism Board *(www.discoverhongkong. com)* gives a broad overview of accommodation online on its hotel directory, which indicates which hotels can be booked online, the price ranges and the number of guestrooms. With more than 5,000 hotel rooms in Hong Kong, you are sure to find something that meets your budget, from luxury hostels to hostels. At the luxury end, expect rooms to start at around HK$4,000, and more for suites. For budget travelers, a bed in a dorm-style room may start as low as HK$150; and there are dozens of guest houses and other low-cost lodgings. For **Youth Hostel Association** rooms or dorm beds, see *www.yha.org.hk*.

Business Hours

Banks & Offices

Banks are generally open Mon–Fri 9am–3pm, Sat 9am–12:30pm and are closed Sundays and public holidays. Most business offices are open Mon–Fri 9am–6pm (lunch hour 1pm–2pm); many open a half-day on Saturdays or alternate Saturdays from 9am–1pm.

Shops

Most shops are open daily. Some shops do not open until 10am or even 11am, but many stay open until 9pm or10pm, or later. In the Central District, a closing time of 8pm–9pm is the rule. Convenience stores such as Circle K and 7-Eleven are open 24/7.

Restaurants and Bars

All but the priciest restaurants are open for lunch and dinner. Bars stay open as long as they have customers, generally until dawn on Fridays, Saturdays and the eves of public holidays.

Attractions

Privately run theme parks and sights are usually open daily. Government museums generally have one weekday that they are closed; check at: *www.lcsd.gov.hk*. Many attractions are closed the first

Buyer Beware

In the 1970s and '80s, Hong Kong was famous for inexpensive electronics, cameras and other consumer goods. That's a thing of the past, but now with a few years of the Hong Kong dollar being a consistently good value for visitors, it is the case again. To avoid being ripped off by inflated price tags, stick to fixed-price chain stores – particularly with electronics; Broadway and Fortress are the two biggest trustworthy names in this arena. Hong Kong is also well known for tailor-made suits, shirts, skirts and dresses at reasonable costs, but take your time choosing which tailor to commission; don't be pressured by the persistent street hawkers in Tsim Sha Tsui and, more recently, in Central.

MUST KNOW

Emergency Services (Police, Fire service or ambulance)	☏**999**
Hospital Authority	☏2300 6555
Dental Emergencies see *www.toothclub.gov.hk* for a list of emergency government dental clinics	☏2713 6344
Current Time & Weather	☏18501
Hong Kong Observatory Weather Forecast	☏1878200
Hong Kong International Airport Information (24 hours)	☏2181 0000

two or three days of the Chinese New Year.

Discounts

Students, children and seniors often get discounts at attractions, restaurants and on public transport; if you are eligible for a discount, you may be asked for personal identification. Consider purchasing an attractions pass (*see sidebar, right*) to save money on entrance fees.

Holidays

Most of Hong Kong comes to something of a standstill during the Chinese New Year, as many shops, banks and offices close during all or part of this period. Supermarkets, convenience stores and many restaurants remain open, though. Banks and offices are generally closed on Christmas, New Years and Easter.

Laws

The public laws of Hong Kong are quite similar to many of those in the West, since they are founded on the British rule of law from colonial days. The territory is one of the safest tourist destinations in the world; there is a zero-tolerance

policy for drugs or arms possession. No smoking, eating or drinking is allowed on public trains and buses, but a blind eye is often turned, especially for beverages in hot weather. No smoking is permitted in any enclosed public places. Fines are handed out for spitting, littering and jaywalking.

Money

The Hong Kong Dollar based on a decimal system and comes in notes of HK$10, 20, 50, 100, 500 and 1,000. Conins come in denominations of 10, 20 and 50 cents, as well as HK$1, $2, $5 and $10. The Hong Kong dollar is pegged to the US dollar at around US$1 to HK$7.80. In mid-2011, HK dollar exchange rates were around HK$12.75 to £1 sterling or

Attractions Pass

www.viator.com. With a choice of 1, 2 or 3 consecutive days, this attractions pass offers free entry to Hong Kong and Macau's most popular attractions, including the Peak Tram, Star Ferry, Macau Tower and many museums. Prices start at HK$51.21 for a 1-day adult pass.

PRACTICAL INFORMATION

HK$11.20 to €1. Hong Kong dollars are interchangeable with the Macau currency, the Pataca (MOP). In Shenzhen, Lo Wu stores will accept Hong Kong dollars and convert them to Renminbi (RMB) on the spot, but taxis and other retailers want RMB, so it may be worth changing your money before crossing the border. In mid-2011, HK$1 = RMB0.84.

Currency Exchange

Licensed money changers operate all of the exchange counters in the main tourist areas and at Chek Lap Kok Airport. The exchange rate fluctuates daily, depending on the market.

© Farang/Dreamstime.com

Credit Cards

All major credit cards are widely accepted in stores, petrol stations and entertainment venues across Hong Kong. You can generally use a credit card everywhere except in very small restaurants, shops and street markets. **Contact numbers for the credit card companies: American Express** – 2277 2180; *www.home.americanexpress.com*. **Diners Club Card** – 2860 1888; *www.dinersclubus.com*. **MasterCard** – 800 966 677 *(toll-free in Hong Kong)*. *www.mastercard.com*.

VISA – 800-900-782 *(toll-free locally). www.visa.com*.

Traveler's Checks

Traveler's checks can be exchanged at all major banks and foreign-exchange outlets. A commission is charged for the service, and you must present a valid passport.

ATMs

The ATM network is extensive, given the number of banks and shopping in the city. Most MTR stations also have ATMs.

Electricity

The electricity system is based on the UK, three-pin flat socket, at 200/220 volts and 50 cycles AC. Non-UK visitors will need an adapter for two-pin plugs.

Internet

The Hong Kong Tourism Board visitor centers offer free Internet access to tourists, as do public libraries. Most large café chains offer a free Wi-Fi connection for their customers.
Visitors can enjoy free Wi-Fi at the Hong Kong Tourist Bureau's website or mobile site via PCCW's 7,000 Wi-Fi Hotspots around the region. For more information, and to download free mobile apps, go to *www.discoverhongkong.com*.

Smoking

Almost all enclosed areas (restaurants, shopping malls, museums, theaters, cinemas) prohibit smoking.
Exceptions can be found in some restaurants and bars that have outdoor areas, a few cigar lounges, and hotels that have smoking floors.

Florent Bonnefoy/Michelin

Information Centres, convenience stores and hotels). Many hotels will charge for local calls made from the rooms.

Area Codes
Hong Kong from abroad: 852
Macau: 853
Mainland China: 86

Useful Numbers
Emergencies: Dial 999
Lost Passport: 2527 7177
(Police hotline)
Hong Kong Directory: 1081
International Directory: 10013
International Operator/
Collect calls: 10010

Time Zone
The entire country of China is in the GMT (Greenwich Mean Time) +8 zone.

Water
It is advisable to carry a bottle of drinking water with you at all times, since the heat and humidity are deceiving and can quickly lead to dehydration. Hong Kong tap water exceeds the World Health Organization standards and is safe to drink.

Taxes and Tips
Hong Kong is a duty-free port; so there is no added tax to pay on goods or to be reclaimed when you leave the country.
Most restaurants and hotels automatically add a 10-percent service charge to bills. It is common to round up restaurant bills to the nearest HK$5 or HK$10; larger tips are expected when no service charge is added.
Taxi fares, too, are often rounded up to the nearest dollar or two as a sufficient tip. Tip restroom attendants and doormen with loose change; HK$10-20 suffices for bellboy and room service.

Telephones
The IDD code is 001, followed by the country code and number. Within Hong Kong, there are no area codes; numbers have eight digits. Pre-paid SIM cards for your mobile phone are widely available in Hong Kong at phone network provider shops, hotel business centers and convenience stores. Coin-operated public telephone kiosks are scarce, but if you do find one, they take coins from HK$1 to HK$10. Many phone kiosks require pre-paid cards (available at HKTB

PEARL OF THE ORIENT

Hong Kong is a small speck at the southern tip of the People's Republic of China (PRC), yet its historical role as a regional trading and financial hub is disproportionately large. After a century and a half of British colonial rule ended, the city was deemed a Special Administrative Region (SAR) in 1997. Today, its rule of law, freedom of speech and a number of other official regulations remain quite different from those north of its border in Mainland China.

Zoom in on this tiny territory of little more than 1,000 square kilometres – around one 16th the size of Beijing – to note that although it is deservedly known for being home to striking skyscrapers and to some of the most densely populated neighborhoods in the world, Hong Kong in many places is wild and uninhabited.

Although home to some 230 islands, the most dense settlements are in the Kowloon Peninsula and Hong Kong Island, with the New Territories (in its upper reaches) and Lantau Island both slowly catching up.

FROM BARREN ROCK TO BUSTLING CITY

Hong Kong's place in history books really starts in 1841 when Hong Kong Island was ceded perpetually to the British crown. Famously referred to as a "barren rock" by British foreign secretary Lord Palmerston at the time, Hong Kong would, of course, become one of the most prosperous free ports in the world. The territory came to include the Kowloon Peninsula in 1860, after the Second Opium War. Finally in 1898, taking advantage of the Japanese victory over China (1894-1895, in a war for the control of the Korean peninsula), the United Kingdom negotiated a further 99-year lease of the territory stretching from Kowloon to the Sham Chun river, as well as more than 200 islands in the China sea.

After the **First Opium War** (1839-1842), Hong Kong suddenly became headquarters for opium traffic to China. In the mid-19th century, the opium trade transformed the handful of fishing villages that spread over this mountainous island.

The colonial government worked with opium traders such as Jardine Matheson, which became the largest company of the colony and played a part in political affairs in Hong Kong until well into the 20th century.

For more than a century, the opium business was at the heart of Hong Kong's existence, attracting thousands of migrants from Guangdong, eager to make their fortunes. Later, after the **Taiping Rebellion** (1850-1864) – led by a converted Christian against the Manchus in power – rich merchants of Guangdong fled to Hong Kong, bringing their trade expertise and contacts with China and Southeast Asia.

POLITICS OF DEMOCRACY

Made up of British commoners and Chinese from the poorer classes, the early population of Hong Kong was atypical to say the least. Colonial discriminations against the Chinese lasted for years, in

The Post-1997 Poser

The most frequent question on the lips of visitors to Hong Kong is: Has it changed much since 1997 when Beijing resumed territorial control?
In truth, very little is different due to sovereignty. Queen Elizabeth II's head disappeared from postage stamps and coins, to be replaced with the symbol of Hong Kong – the bauhinia flower – on coins. And red post boxes had their royal crests removed and were painted green. However, Victoria Harbour and Park are still so-named, after the reigning British queen at the start of the colonial period; and countless streets and buildings retain their references to British colonial governors and officials. Signage and official spoken languages are still Cantonese and English.
Hong Kong appoints its own government through a closed internal process – which is also how it was done under British rule. Beijing is not directly involved in this. There are movements afoot for democratic elections to vote in Hong Kong's government and Chief Executive – these were slated for 2012, but at the time of this writing, Beijing has delayed this from happening.

spite of the rise of a singular class of merchants called compradors. They served as middlemen in the People's Republic of China (PRC) for the trade of western companies. The colonial government, although worried over the compradors' influence, ended up involving them in political affairs in order to maintain control over the local population. Some compradors even became noblemen and became members of the Legislative Council.

From the start, the colony enjoyed a legal system that protected the rights inherent to free exchange – property, individual rights and freedom of expression. So it is no surprise that revolutionaries and reformists found asylum in Hong Kong when they faced a reversal of fortune in Mainland China. **Sun Yat-sen**, who studied medi-

Royal Navy March in Hong Kong in 1937

cine there, came back to launch Anti-Manchuist movements. Communists found refuge in Hong Kong after the Kuomintang declared Communism illegal in China in 1927. Intellectuals arrived from Shanghai after the Second Sino-Japanese War in 1937. Since the creation of the PRC, some of the partisans of Kuomintang and victims of various political campaigns, including those of the Cultural Revolution in the 1970s and the Tiananmen protests and massacres of 1989, have found asylum in Hong Kong. Surprisingly, in 1949, the Communists, who were conquering China at the expense of the Nationalists, stopped their advance on the north bank of the Sham Chun River, leaving the colony intact – in spite of the mark the unfair treaties had left in the collective memory. Cut off from the continent, Hong Kong flourished after the return of the part of its population that had fled during the Japanese invasion (1941-1945).

After World War II, the struggles between Communists and Nationalists would also drive thousands of Chinese to flee to the territory. Migrants became a source of cheap labor that would help line the pockets of local entrepreneurs. This spelled the rise of the "Made in Hong Kong" era fueled by the textile and toy industries. But the policy of economic openness initiated by PRC Vice Premier **Deng Xiaoping** in 1979 would bring Hong Kong-based investments back to South China and lead to the relocation of factories on cheaper land, leaving Hong Kong to become a center of financial and regional logistics services.

While Great Britain may have hoped that a new lease with China could be possible, Deng Xiaoping was not going to let go of the golden egg that was Hong Kong. Determined to recuperate the area, he applied a theory called "one country, two systems" to Hong Kong. The capitalist system was to remain unchanged in Hong Kong for 50 years.

The **Sino-British Joint Declaration** that laid the foundations for the future SAR

Hong Kong Skyline

Hong Kong Facts

Area: 1,108sq km/428sq mi

Population: 7.1 million

Annual visitors: More than 30 million

Year of reverting to Chinese rule: 1997

Form of government: Self-appointed limited democracy

Airlines servicing Chek Lap Kok Airport: 95

Official languages: Cantonese and English.

Population density: 6,054.5 inhabitants/sq km, with Mong Kok holding the world record at 130,000 inhabitants/sq km.

was signed on December 19, 1984. Seeing the end of the colonial period approaching and the anxiety of the Hong Kongese widening, Chris Patten, the last governor, launched a series of hasty reforms intended to establish a democracy. His measures led to the first universal suffrage elections for Hong Kong deputies in 1995. China accused Britain of interfering and, in 1997, it dissolved the assembly and replaced it with Beijing partisans.

THE CITY TODAY

A place more concerned with material well-being, Hong Kong sometimes seems as if it is overrun with shopping malls. And while Hong Kongers today are not deeply political, the call to democracy is often heard, and protests over dissidents detained on the Mainland are common. Hong Kong is one of the safest places in the world, with no off-limits areas, so feel free to turn off the glitzy main roads in the popular tourist zones of the Central District on Hong Kong Island and Tsim Sha Tsui into side streets and smaller lanes to get a feel of the real Hong Kong.

Shrines bearing offerings of fruit and incense sticks, some lit daily, dot many an office building doorway; inside smaller shops and restaurants, owners also display deities believed to protect and bring good fortune to the premises.

Outside the heavily touristed areas, expect restaurants and cafés to have Chinese-only menus (and, in some, to speak mainly Chinese). Foreign faces are common in Hong Kong, so if you see something you'd like to try – in an open kitchen at the front of a restaurant, as many of them tend to be, or on a nearby diner's table – just point at it, nod to a waiter and sit yourself down. Neighborhood restaurants are good spots for observing the locals, often animated in their conversation, whether with companions or on their mobile phones.

Despite the invasion of Western-style gadgets and shopping malls, the territory still clings to many of the old Chinese ways. As you travel around the region, you'll see evidence of this all around you, in the many dim sum restaurants, traditional Chinese medicine shops, and historic temples.

PEARL OF THE ORIENT

REGIONS

One of two special administrative regions (SARs) of the People's Republic of China (the other is Macau), Hong Kong is geographically divided into several distinct regions. Hong Kong Island claims the territory's seat of government and the center of finance, while, across Victoria Harbour, the peninsula of Kowloon lays out a dense landscape of hotels, restaurants and residential and commercial areas, as well as some of the area's best museums. Beyond Kowloon, the New Territories occupy the landmass north of Boundary Street in Kowloon and south of the Sham Chun River, which forms the border with Mainland China.

HONG KONG ISLAND NORTH

From some of the world's most striking modern architecture to mazes of small backstreets filled with the market stalls of yore, on the north side of Hong Kong Island you'll discover a concentration of some of the last intact historic buildings in the territory, as well as a crazy quilt of contrasting neighborhoods that quickly morph from historic to modern and from international to traditional Southern Chinese. Take time to wander the streets where the first British colonists settled and named the central district Victoria City, thus transforming the island into the political and economic heart of the colony. The farther east and west from Central you go, the more densely populated the residential cum commercial communities become.

Central★★ 中環

Central ranks as Hong Kong Island's north shore hub, a core business district peppered with swanky shops and restaurants and home to **Lan Kwai Fong**, a popular quarter for nightlife. East of Central you'll find the malls and parks of **Admiralty**, and beyond, **Wan Chai**, a neighborhood primarily composed of offices and hotels but also home to a vibrant

From Star Ferry Pier to Statue Square

If you are staying in Kowloon, Star Ferry boats can take you from Tsim Sha Tsui pier to the pier in Central in seven minutes. If you are staying on Hong Kong Island, the **Star Ferry Pier** is a good starting point for a walk around Central. Constructed in neo-Edwardian style in 2006, this pier replaced the original 1957 structure, in spite of public efforts to preserve it.

For excursions to the Outlying Islands, you'll find the **Outer Island Ferry Piers** (see Excursions) right next to the Central Star Ferry. You can reach **Statue Square★** (opposite page) by one of the many **overhead walkways** that crisscross Central. Pass by the **IFC Mall**, whose office tower – the highest in the district – soars to 420m/1,378 ft (there is no public observation tower here). Many buses that run on the island start and terminate under **Exchange Square**, next to the mall. The IFC Mall tower houses the Hong Kong Stock Exchange, one of the largest financial centers in the world.

Central Business District

Hong Kong Tourism Board

nightlife scene. **Causeway Bay** is the favorite shopping and dining area of many a Hong Konger and is always abuzz. On the other side of Victoria Park, **Happy Valley** holds the territory's famed city racetrack. To the west of Hong Kong Island north, **Sheung Wan** lies only a few minutes walk from Central, but its old Chinese ambience feels far removed.

Tower after tower, constantly changing, Central rises ever higher between the sea and Victoria Peak. It's not always easy to find your way when you're surrounded by skyscrapers or in the middle of the labyrinth of glitzy shopping malls that are linked together by elevated pedestrian passages. But the district is well worth exploring, as much for its extravagant modern architectural achievements—evident in the giant glass, steel and cement towers—as for the handful of colonial buildings of British influence that still stand. Central's landmarks are mostly skyscrapers – **Two IFC** (International Finance Centre), **Exchange Square**, and the real structural icons, **HSBC**

Tower★★ and **Bank of China Tower★★** (see Skyscrapers). This was once the hub of the City of Victoria; that moniker was dropped in the early 20C, when Central and a string of other small districts that lay within its boundaries took on their own names as population and urban development mushroomed. Little of the colonial era remains today, but you can still glimpse vestiges of this era at the **Legislative Council (LegCo) Building**, **Saint John's Cathedral★**, and by peeking through the gates of the old colonial governor's residence, **Government House** (see Colonial Sites).

Top-tier Chinese and Western restaurants are scattered throughout the district in hotels and in some of the upscale malls; a more boisterous district for food and drink can be found in Lan Kwai Fong's executive party zone, or in more laid-back style, in intimate establishments mixed among the ever-increasing small boutiques of the SoHo district, which borders art galleries and antique shops on Hollywood Road.

39

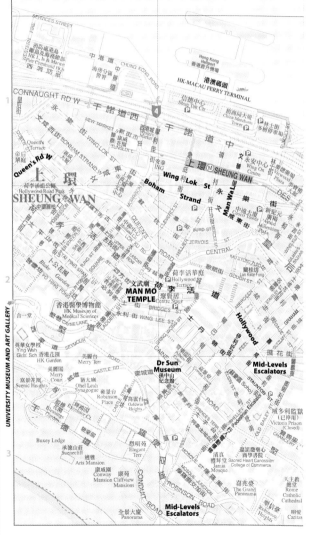

中環（中區）
CENTRAL DISTRICT

SERVICES STREET

消防處港島
總區及西消防局
H.K. Is. & West
Fire Command HQ
西消防局

中港道 CHUNG KONG ROAD
海傍分區
警署

Hong Kong
Heliport
香港直升機場

CONNAUGHT RD W 干諾道西
NEW MARKET ST
新街市街

HK-MACAU FERRY TERMINAL
港澳碼頭

信德中心
Shun Tak Ctr.

招商局大廈
China Merchants
Tower

干諾道中

永安中心
Wing On
Centre

林士街
多層停車場

Queen's Rd W
皇后大道西

Queen's Terrace
帝后
華庭

BONHAM STRAND W 文咸東街
永樂西街
WING LOK ST
永樂街
TUNG LO ST

上環 ⓂSHEUNG WAN

DES

荷李活道公園
Hollywood Road Park
上環文娛中心

Wing Lok St

永和街

Man Wa Lane

新紀元廣場
Grand
Millennium
Plaza

SHEUNG WAN
上環

Bonham

Strand

QUEEN'S
LOK KU ROAD
文武廟
LADDER

CENTRAL
KAU U FONG

蘭桂坊
Lan Kwai Fong

HILLIER ST
JERVOIS ST

上亞厘畢街

Hollywood
荷李活華庭
Hollywood
Centre

Centre St

MAN MO
TEMPLE
文武廟

LADDER ST
PO HING FONG

Blake
Garden
卜公花園

永利街
WING LEE ST

荷李活道

Hollywood

GRAHAM ST

伊利近街

香港醫學博物館
HK Museum of
Medical Sciences

CAINE LANE

BRIDGES ST

十字路

擺花街
PEEL ST

CAINE

英華女學校
Ying Wah
Girls' Sch

香港花園
HK Garden

美麗台
Merry Terr

ROAD

Dr Sun
Museum
孫中山
紀念館

Mid-Levels
Escalators

STAUNTON ST

多利監獄
（已停用）
Victoria Prison
(Closed)

CASTLE RD

CHANCERY L

OLD BAILEY

美麗閣
Merry
Court

劉太廟
Ohel Leah
Synagogue

羅便臣道
Robinson
Place

SEYMOUR

PRINCES TERR

SOHO

雲咸街

雪廠街

Pedestrian Escalator

ROBINSON

富麗花園
Scenic Heights

高雲軒
Goldwin
Heights

嘉諾撒聖心
商學院
Sacred Heart Canossian
College of Commerce

ROAD

Blessing
Garden

教堂台

Buxey Lodge

承德山莊
Suenecliff

迦雅
Arts Mansion

康威園
Conway
Mansion

康苑
Cliffview
Mansions

明麗苑
Elegant
Terr

MOSQUE
清真
禮拜總堂
Jamia
Mosque

MOSQUE JUNCTION

ROBINSON

嘉兆臺
The Grand
Panorama

ROAD

天主教
總堂
Rome
Catholic
Cathedral

明愛
Caritas

CONDUIT

全景大廈
Panorama

Mid-Levels
Escalators

Robinson
Heights

40

216m

N

1號碼頭 Pier 1
2號碼頭 Pier 2
往愉景灣 To Discovery Bay
往赤柱 To Park Island
3號碼頭 Pier 3
往榕樹灣 To Yung Shue Wan
4號碼頭 Pier 4
往索罟灣 To So Kwu Wan
往長洲 To Cheung Chau
5號碼頭 Pier 5
往坪洲 To Peng Chau
6號碼頭 Pier 6
7號碼頭 Pier 7
往梅窩 To Mui Wo
往尖沙咀 To Tsim

天星碼頭
Star Ferry Pier

MAN PO ST
MAN CHIU ST
民光街
民耀街
民寶街
民業街

民 耀 街 MAN KWONG STREET

政府總部 Harbour Building
民 金 街 MAN KAM ST

四季酒店
Four Seasons Hotel

MAN PO ST

FINANCE ST STREET

CONNAUGHT RD C
VOEUX RD C
JUBILEE ST

P 停車場

國際金融中心商場
IFC Mall

國際金融中心二期
Two International Finance Centre

中環中心
The Center

中環街市
Central Market

MAN CHEUNG ST
HARBOUR VIEW ST
MAN YIU ST

MAN YEE ARCADE

Mid-Levels Escalators

QUEEN VICTORIA ST

香港 HONG KONG

IFC Mall

交易廣場
Exchange 2 Square

郵政總局
General Post Office

POTTINGER ST
U LYEN STW
DOUGLAS ST

遮打花園 Chater Garden

Road

LYNDHURST TERR
WELLINGTON ST
STANLEY ST

怡和大廈
Jardine House

CENTRAL
中環

M 中環 CENTRAL

B 打

歷山大廈
Alexandra House

遮 打 道 CHATER RD

置地廣場
Landmark

太子大廈
Prince's Building

文華東方
Mandarin Oriental

CONNAUGHT RD C

Statue Square
皇后像廣場

WYNDHAM ST
LAN KWAI FONG
QUEENS ROAD
DUDDELL ST

雪廠街
Ice House St

置地廣場
Landmark

文華東方
The Galleria

CENTRAL BATTERY

中環
CENTRAL

匯豐總行大廈
HSBC Tower

中國銀行大廈
Bank of China Tower

長江集團中心
Cheung Kong Center

DEVOUX ST
D'AGUILAR ST
ARBUTHNOT RD
GLENEALY
WYNDHAM ST

ALBANY RD

CENTRAL HEALTH MEDICAL PRACTICE

Church Guest Hse

終審法院
Court of Final Appeal

聖約翰座堂
St. John's Cathedral

HONG KONG PARK

ZOOLOGICAL AND BOTANICAL GARDENS

Statue Square★ 皇后像廣場

Queen's Road. MTR: Central.

This lovely landscaped plaza, with its fountains, pools and plantings, provides a welcome respite in the heart of the city. The name comes from the statues of Queen Victoria, Prince Albert and King Edward VII that stood here during British colonial days. (The Japanese removed the statues during World War II.) Today, the square's current statue depicts **Sir Thomas Jackson** (1841–1915), director of the Hong Kong and Shanghai Bank (HSBC). He made HSBC the first bank of Asia at the end of the 19C. Surrounding Statue Square are the Mandarin Oriental hotel (*see Hotels*) and the **Legislative Council Building**, which houses the institution charged with enacting the island's laws. On the roof of this 1912 neoclassically inspired building, the flag of the People's Republic of China waves next to the flag of Hong Kong. The latter features a white *Bauhinia blakeana* flower (the bloom of a native tree) against a red background.

Sheung Wan and Mid-Levels★★★ 上環與半山區

A step away from the financial hub, the western districts were occupied by the British in the beginning of the colonial period. Old market stalls, antique shops and medicinal herb stores line many of the streets here. Revelers tired of the superficiality of Lan Kwai Fong in Central flock to the hip streets of SoHo (South of Hollywood Road). Modern art galleries have opened on the western end of Hollywood Road, and in the Mid-Levels, where expatriates and wealthier Hong Kong Chinese occupy some of the most expensive apartments on the island.

Central to the Mid-Levels Escalators★ 中環至半山自動扶梯

Starting point on Des Voux Rd., joining Central Market; jump off at various points through SoHo, as it follows Cochrane Street. MTR: Central.

Central to the Mid-Levels Escalators

Florent Bonnefoy/Michelin

A good way to discover part of the district is by traveling on the giant escalators, which facilitate the steep climb from Central to the residential area of the Mid-Levels. The world's longest covered escalator (800m/2,600ft) runs downhill until 10:15am, and then goes into climbing mode for the rest of the day.

Escalators pass by SoHo and the fresh produce stands and food stalls of the **Graham Street Market** (*Graham and Peel Sts.*). SoHo's intimate cafés and bars are concentrated around Staunton and Elgin streets.

Hollywood Road★★ 荷李活道

MTR: Central.

From the Mid-Levels escalators, get off at Hollywood Road, where you

Eastern Traditions of Well-Being

Open shopfronts along Queen's Road West and Wing Lok Street in the Sheung Wan and Western districts offer a typical taste, and, often, smell, of Hong Kong's dried foods and herbal medicine products.

Displays are piled high with the likes of dried mushroom and wood fungi (destined for the dinner table), side by side with roots, berries, fruits, seahorses and insect shells, which are taken home and boiled by customers according to the prescriptions of a traditional Chinese herbalist. Some of the stores along Queen's Road West and Wing Lok Street offer these products at wholesale rates; but like many businesses in Hong Kong, these shops are just as happy to make retail sales. Good-quality herbal medicines and supplements can be found at Chinese Department stores, such as **Yue Hwa** (*301-309 Nathan Rd., Jordan, Kowloon; 2611 9622*).

Some smaller shops employ a qualified **traditional Chinese medicine** (TCM) practitioner. If you are interested in a consultation, you'll need the help of a Chinese speaker to fully understand the diagnosis and recommendations. Standard procedure is to describe your symptoms and let the herbalist feel the pulse of both wrists and your outstretched tongue. The practitioner (they are predominantly male) will then consider all this information along with his assessment of your general demeanor, and prescribe an oral herbal remedy. For the visitor, it is best to get the powdered form that can be mixed into hot water, rather than the larger traditional packs of dried ingredients that must be boiled for an hour or so at home. As is the case with all natural medicine, do not expect a quick fix; follow-up appointments are advised.

can browse antique shops by the dozen. These offer objects from all over Asia (the prices are rather high in the first boutiques you come to, but the farther west along Hollywood Road you go, the more reasonable the prices become). **Upper Lascar Road**, also known as "Cat Street" (*see Shopping*) harbors shops full of "vintage" souvenirs. (Buyer beware that many of these tchotchkes actually come from factories in Guangdong, which specialize in making new items look old.) Named for the woods of holly that once covered this area, Hollywood Road runs all the way to Central. Along the way, it crosses Possession Street, where the English planted the Union Jack on January 26, 1841.

Bonham Strand★★ 文咸街
MTR: Sheung Wan.
This district within a district is among the most typically Chinese in the city. Along **Man Hwa Lane**, seal engravers (*see Local Crafts*) have set up their stalls. These seals bear the name of their owner, carved in stone or bone in high- or low-relief.

Queen's Road West and **Wing Lok Street** are a paradise for practitioners of Chinese medicine – and a horror show for defenders of animal rights. Dried shellfish, fungi and "swallow's nests" (actually the saliva the birds use to anchor their nests to rocky cliff walls) are all highly prized in local cuisine. Used to cure any number of serious ailments – and a key ingredient in a popular soup – sharks' fins are one of the most coveted and controversial products, given the danger that this type of commerce represents for shark populations.

Victoria Peak★★★
太平山

Funicular railway leaves every 10–15min from 7am–12am; HK$40 round-trip. The lower terminus is on Garden Rd., opposite Saint John's Cathedral. Or take bus no.15 from Exchange Square, Central. www.thepeak.com.hk.

Now known as The Peak, Victoria Peak, boasts some of the most luxurious residences of the island. At the beginning of the colonial period, the well-heeled moved here to get away from the heat of the seashore. The **Peak Tram** has been running since 1884, built by a hotel owner to transport guests up the mountain more quickly and comfortably than in sedan chairs. In 1888 the funicular railway was opened to the public. At the summit (552m/1,811 ft) the **view** is spectacular, by day or by night.

Peak Tower

Hong Kong Tourism Board

There's also a popular loop trail that takes about an hour to walk. Weather permitting, you may even catch a glimpse of the New Territories in the distance.

Peak Tower★ 凌霄閣
Open year-round Mon–Fri 10am–11pm, Sat, Sun & holidays 8am–11pm. 2849 0668. www.thepeak.com. hk.
Built in 1972 and redeveloped twice since then (most recently in 2006), this contemporary bowl-shaped landmark is home to restaurants, souvenir shops and the **Sky Terrace** (HK$30). The latter affords a panoramic 360-degree view of the island and its surroundings, and has a panel display relating to the island's historical highlights.
Also in the tower is a **Madame Tussaud's** museum, with wax figures depicting local and international celebrities *(2849 6966; www.madametussauds.com/hongkong; open daily 10am–10pm; HK$160).*

Wan Chai 灣仔
Located east of Central, Wan Chai is a district in the midst of redevelopment. During the Korean and Vietnam wars, American soldiers on leave overran this quarter. Though some go-go bars dating back to those days remain between Lockhart and Jaffe roads, today the area is known for its trendy international restaurants and bars, which bustle with activity until the wee hours of the morning. Looming 374m/1,227ft over Wan Chai, **Central Plaza** office tower boasts a great view from its 46th-floor **observatory**, which is open to the public. Hong

ISLAND NORTH

MUST SEE

Kongers, always ready to poke fun at new construction, nicknamed Central Plaza "the Big Syringe."

Hong Kong Convention and Exhibition Centre
香港會議覽中心
11 Expo Dr. 2582 8888. www.hkcec. com.hk. MTR: Wan Chai.

Hong Kong Convention and Exhibition Centre

Hong Kong Tourism Board

The enormous waterfront convention center complex was the site of the official transfer of sovereignty of Hong Kong; you can visit the lobby where the ceremony took place. Outside, a black obelisk commemorates the event. Today the Centre hosts major conventions, exhibits, fairs and even food expos. A flag-raising ceremony—with both the flags of the PRC and Hong Kong—takes place every morning at 7:50am, to the sounds of the national anthem of the People's Republic.

Causeway Bay 銅鑼灣

MTR: Causeway Bay.

Comprising department stores, apartment buildings, restaurants and hip independent boutiques, this district just east of Wan Chai was built on land reclaimed from the bay. Easily accessible by the "ding ding" (as Hong Kong's tram is locally known), the district is prized by window-shoppers who delight in malls like towering **Times Square** (*see Shopping*), with its nine stories of retail space.

Typhoon Shelter 避風塘
Across from the World Trade Centre, access by pedestrian underpass. MTR: Causeway Bay.
Negotiate a tour of the small boat mooring by sampan to get another view of Causeway Bay. A walk along the Typhoon Shelter quay hints at old maritime Hong Kong, far from the consumer madness of Causeway Bay and Wan Chai. The **Noonday Gun**, a 19C cannon, goes off every day; it once belonged to the Jardine Company, who used it to announce the arrival of its opium cargo boats. The governor at the time, who was annoyed that cannons should be publicly used to honor someone other than himself, ordered the cannon be fired every day at noon. From the Typhoon Shelter, it's a short walk to **Victoria Park** (*see Parks and Gardens*).

Happy Valley 跑馬地

MTR: Causeway Bay; or take the tram to Happy Valley terminus.
See Horse Racing.

Once a mosquito-infested marshland, Happy Valley is an affluent residential neighborhood today. Unless you have an interest in cemeteries of departed colonial figures and members of Hong Kong's non-Chinese communities – the area provides for several different faiths – the chief reason for visiting this quarter is the **Happy Valley Racecourse** (*Wong Nai Chung Rd.; 1817; www.hkjc.com*).

REGIONS

HONG KONG ISLAND SOUTH

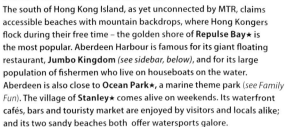

The south of Hong Kong Island, as yet unconnected by MTR, claims accessible beaches with mountain backdrops, where Hong Kongers flock during their free time – the golden shore of **Repulse Bay★** is the most popular. Aberdeen Harbour is famous for its giant floating restaurant, **Jumbo Kingdom** (*see sidebar, below*), and for its large population of fishermen who live on houseboats on the water. Aberdeen is also close to **Ocean Park★**, a marine theme park (*see Family Fun*). The village of **Stanley★** comes alive on weekends. Its waterfront cafés, bars and touristy market are enjoyed by visitors and locals alike; and its two sandy beaches both offer watersports galore.

Aberdeen★ 香港仔

Buses 70 and 75 from Exchange Square, Central.

Built on a bay that was home to Tanka and Hoklo (peoples from Fujian) fishermen before the British colonization, Aberdeen ranks as the island's second-largest urban center. Framed by concrete towers, the port is an attraction in itself, crammed with wooden fishing boats – many of them live-aboard vessels, home to many families. The little arbor at Aberdeen is actually a typhoon shelter, protecting sampans from the storms that regularly occur between May and September. Here, a wholesale **seafood market** operates each morning, and impromptu sales might be seen at any time of day when fishermen return with their catch. Fishermen often dry their catch in shallow baskets or string it on lines, to be sold later along the harbor wall. **Sampan tours** of the little harbor are offered by persistent elderly women who trade on the fact that tourists are normally easy marks. That said, a sampan tour is actually quite an enjoyable experience. Expect to pay around HK$100 for about 15–20 minutes of puttering around the fisher-family boats and the newer pleasure vessels moored in the harbor.

If you cross the road on one of the pedestrian footbridges that take you away from the water, you can grab some dim sum or noodles in one of the modest establishments in Aberdeen's compact commercial center. Look over toward the hills, and you can see the cable cars of **Ocean Park★** transporting passengers up a steep grade.

Jumbo Kingdom

In Aberdeen Harbour; accessible by shuttle boat from Aberdeen Promenade. 2553-9111. www.jumbo.com.hk. Styled like a Chinese Imperial palace, this huge floating restaurant has presided over Aberdeen Harbour for some 30 years. It may not be the most authentic place to eat, but it's still fun to dine on Cantonese fare like roasted Peking duck and the signature flamed drunken shrimp – prepared tableside – while enjoying a perch on the water. The **Top Deck** on Jumbo's roof dishes up Western fare. To get here, follow the harbor to the jetty and catch one of the restaurant's free shuttles.

Jumbo Kingdom

Small wooden ferries called *kaidos* run from Aberdeen to the little village of **Yung Shue Wan** on **Lamma Island**★ (*see Excursions*), a laid-back place to spend time and sample some fresh seafood meal before returning to the bustle of Central.

The Beach Route★ 沙灘之路

Buses 6, 6A, and 260 from Exchange Square, Central.

The bus ride to the beaches is a pleasant escape past the high rises of Hong Kong through the lower-rise pockets of the territory, all of them exclusive residential zones.

Deep Water Bay★ 深水灣
See Beaches.
Once you pass through Aberdeen Tunnel, the road hugs a winding road that leads to Deep Water Bay.

Repulse Bay★ 淺水灣
See Beaches.
Close by is the longer and busier beach at Repulse Bay, which is particularly popular on weekends.

Stanley★ 赤柱

Buses 6, 6A, 6X and 260 from Exchange Square, Central.

A half-hour bus ride from Central, the Mediterranean-looking low-rise village of Stanley appeals for its sandy beaches and lively restaurants and bars.
Folks flock here on weekends and public holidays. Unfortunately, the former fishing village today – half a century after it was re-developed bears little evidence of its history.
Along the waterfront, the wooden-decked **Stanley Promenade** boasts a string of open-front restaurants and bars. Nearby, you can buy everything from kitschy souvenirs to swimwear in the jumble of stalls at **Stanley Market** Follow Stanley Main Road to **Murray House**, (*See Colonial Sites*). Close by is **Tin Hau Temple**, said to date back to 1767.
Swimmers, wind surfers and jet-skiers favor **Stanley Main Beach** and the prettier **St. Stephen's Beach** for their calm waters (*see Beaches*).

KOWLOON 九龍

This narrow peninsula at the southern tip of Victoria Harbour takes its name from the gau lung ("nine dragons" in Cantonese), a reference to the range of rugged mountain peaks that form the area's backdrop. Kowloon widens considerably before giving way to the New Territories to its north (which extend centrally to Lion Rock and to Kowloon Peak in the east). At the southernmost tip is **Tsim Sha Tsui★★**, on a piece of land that has been reclaimed from the sea. It is bordered by Austin Road to the north and Hung Hom station to the east. This is one of the most vibrant areas of Hong Kong, and where you'll find some of the city's finest museums.

With its giant neon signs, restaurants and stores, **Nathan Road★★★** traverses Tsim Sha Tsui from north to south. North of Tsim Sha Tsui, between Austin Road and Dundas Street, is **Yau Ma Tei**, one of the first areas to develop after the British colonized Kowloon, and site of the venerable **Tin Hau Temple★★★** (see Temples). For a moment of quiet contemplation, head here or to the gardens and prayer halls of **Chi Lin Nunnery★★★** (see Heritage Sites).

Some expatriates dismissingly consider Kowloon to be the dark side of Hong Kong and they make it a point to avoid the place. This attitude may stem from the territorial schism that has prevailed since the colonial period: the British occupied Hong Kong Island, while the Chinese population was concentrated on the mainland. Kowloon still is not as glamorous as Central, although pockets of it have been recently gentrified. Relatively noisy and crawling with people in some areas – such as **Mong Kok**, which has one of the densest populations on earth – Kowloon is one of the most authentically atmospheric parts of the modern territory.

Tsim Sha Tsui★★ 尖沙咀

Today no traces remain of the sandy, peninsular character brought to mind by the Cantonese name for Tsim Sha Tsui, which means "Pointed Sandy Mouth." Concrete has long since taken over, and, little by little, polders

Nathan Road

© Typhoonski/Dreamstime.com

Stars of the Orient

A statue of Bruce Lee marks the beginning of the **Avenue of Stars**★ 星光大道 (*MTR: Tsim Sha Tsui*), created in 2004 and modeled on Hollywood's Walk of Fame. Handprints of several celebrities from Hong Kong's movie industry are set in cement here, including actors Jackie Chan, Maggie Cheung and Jet Li; and directors John Woo, Tsui Hark and Wong Kar-Wai. Embedded in the ground between the brass stars and the handprints are lights that change color for some added underfoot pizzazz. While all of the names here may not be familiar to the Western traveler, they are well known to Asian visitors. Thus this strip is often packed with those seeking photo opportunities, particularly just before dusk, when the tour groups arrive.

have encroached on the bay. While some people prefer Hong Kong hands-down, others love Tsim Sha Tsui and its shopping centers. Indeed, it is difficult to find such a concentration of name brands anywhere in the world, but there is so much more to Tsim Sha Tsui than that.

Nathan Road★★★
梳士巴利道與彌敦道
MTR station: Tsim Sha Tsui.
Nathan Road is the main north-to-south thoroughfare of Kowloon, stretching from Tsim Sha Tsui to Boundary Street in the Prince Edward District – which marked the border of China at the time when the New Territories were not yet part of the colony.

The energy along Nathan Road pulsates: enormous neon signs hang down from the building façades, while hawkers for tailors and factory outlets compete with the wares of overflowing shopfronts and occasional cart peddlers for your money. Restaurants run into stores – every inch of space is exploited here. And the crowds aren't fazed one bit by the traffic and pollution as they seek out bargains or a good restaurant.

On the corner of **Kowloon Park** (*See Parks and Gardens*) stands the **Jamia Masjid and Islamic Centre** (*closed to the public*), with its imposing dome and minaret. Built in 1984, the mosque replaced for the original 19C house of worship built for the British Indian military.

Today, it is the main mosque for Kowloon's Muslim population, half of which is Chinese.

Seafront Promenade★★
海濱花園
Salisbury Rd. MTR: Tsim Sha Tsui.
Edging this little cultural quarter is a quayside promenade, which continues to the **Avenue of Stars**★ (*see sidebar, below*).
The promenade offers the best view of the 10-minute **Symphony of Lights**, which occurs nightly at 8pm; this spectacle has come under fire recently for being environmentally unfriendly, but for now the laser show continues. Across the harbor on Hong Kong Island, the skyscrapers of the Central district light up in a wonderland of neon that is reflected in the water after dusk. This view is equally impressive on a clear day.

Fortune Readings

As western as Hong Kong may at times seem, among its many actively practiced Southern Chinese traditions are the superstitions based on Buddhist temple culture. At **Yue Shau Tau Square**, the grounds around the **Tin Hau Temple★★★** in Yau Ma Tei (*See Temples*), fill with fortune tellers and feng shui masters in the evening. Every method of prediction known to the Chinese culture is used, from reading the lines of one's face to the interpretation of bird calls. Western techniques, such as tarot and astrology, are also practiced by a few of the pyschics.

At a few temples around the territory, you will see people shaking bamboo sticks in long bamboo cups in hopes of divining their future. When one of the sticks works itself to the top and falls to the floor, the person notes the character engraved on the end and takes it to one of the many mediums onsite. They then interpret its meaning with the aid of a traditional almanac. **Wong Tai Sin Temple★★★** (*See Temples*) in Kowloon is one establishment where this takes place on a large scale.

Chunking Mansions 重慶大廈
36-44 Nathan Rd. MTR: Tsim Sha Tsui. www.chungking-mansions.hk.

This 17-story warren of alleys, elevators, cheap guesthouses, shops, and Indian and African restaurants was erected as a residential complex in 1961. Comprising five blocks, the Mansions are still home to a sizeable ethnic population. Backpackers come here for the cheap accommodations, and this is a good place to dine on authentic curry dishes. Don't be surprised to see a gathering of hustler types at the entrance to the Mansions.

Salisbury Road Museums
梳士巴利道與彌敦道

Salisbury Road leads to Hung Hom Station; to the west, it crosses Nathan Road. At the road's head, opposite The Peninsula hotel – where the stylish international travel set have met up in the lobby since the1920s (*see Hotels*) – are two museums of note: the **Hong Kong Museum of Art★★★** (*see Cultural Museums*), and **Hong Kong Space Museum** (*see Family Fun*). These both lie within a few paces of the **Hong Kong Cultural Centre** (*see Performing Arts*). Tsim Sha Tsui East is also home to two other museums that are popular with children, the **Hong Kong Science Museum** (*see Family Fun*) and the nearby **Hong Kong Museum of History★★★** (*on Chatham Rd. South; see Cultural Museums*), which appeals to visitors of all ages.

Yau Ma Tei and Mong Kok★★ 旺角與油麻地

Most famous for the markets that border Yau Ma Tei's southern fringes with the Jordan District and the northern limits in Mong Kok, these two neighborhoods represent a typically gritty slice of Kowloon. The **Jade Market★** (*see Street Markets*) at the corner of Kansu and Shanghai streets spreads over two hangars. The polished semi-precious green gem sold here is highly prized in southern China and believed to

The Triad

Originally the Heaven and Earth Society, the Triad is a secret organization founded by Shaolin Monks who had survived the persecution of the Qing. It was built on an ideology consisting of Taoist, Buddhist and Manichaeist beliefs and included defectors from the ruling classes.

After 1949, the Triad fled to Hong Kong and overseas, abandoning their revolutionary ideals for more lucrative illegal activities: drug trafficking, prostitution and counterfeiting.

Jade Market, Kowloon

© Florent Bonnefoy/Michelin

and south, and Jordan Road to the north, is currently slated to become the West Kowloon Cultural District. Debate on how and when this will happen has gone on for years and is not yet finalized. To date, two hotels and a new observation deck (below) are the first attractions to appear in the vicinity.

be endowed with protective and lucky properties. Jade is carved into every conceivable shape in rings, bracelets, pendants and much more.

The **Temple Street Night Market★★★** (open 2pm–10pm; see Street Markets) wakes up when the sun goes down. You'll find a bit of everything being sold here, from electronic gadgets to kitschy souvenirs. Be sure to check the products before you buy; not all the merchandise here is authentic. Follow Tung Choi Street south beyond Argyle Street to the the **Ladies Market** (see Street Markets), which despite its name, is not just reserved for women.

West Kowloon
西九龍文娛藝術區

This large swath of reclaimed land bounded by Canton Road to the east, Victoria Harbour to the west

Sky 100 天際100

International Commerce Centre, 1 Austin Rd. MTR: Central. Open year-round daily 10am–10pm (last tickets sold at 9pm). HK$150 (HK$125 if purchased in advance online). www.sky100.com.hk.

Take an elevator ride to the 100th floor of the International Commerce Centre (see Skyscrapers) – the tallest building in Hong Kong – for a stellar 360-degree view of the area. The ride takes only 60 seconds, and the elevator is equipped with LED sky panels and multi-lingual commentary. On the sky deck, you'll find intelligent video telescopes, multimedia exhibits detailing Hong Kong history and culture, and enormous touch-screen information boards that provide regional touring tips. For easy access, you can download data from the information boards and email it to yourself.

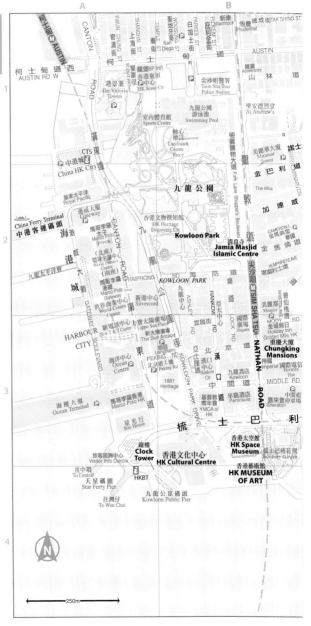

維多利亞港
VICTORIA HARBOUR

尖沙咀
TSIM SHA TSUI

NEW TERRITORIES 新界

Officially, the New Territories stretch from northern Kowloon to the Sham Chun river (the border with Mainland China), and occupy some 90 percent of Hong Kong's landmass. In their upper and most westerly and easterly regions, they remain green rural areas, and natural parks have been established through much of the vicinity. **The Sai Kung peninsula is a popular day trip** – bear it in mind if you are fond of hiking and seafood restaurants. Several new towns were built in the New Territories beginning in the 1970s to accommodate the overflow of residents from some of the more densely populated areas. Among these, **Sha Tin★**, to the east, with its museums and temples, is one of the more interesting. The New Territories also include the 230-plus islands known as the **Outlying Islands** *(see Excursions)*.

Clear Water Bay and Sai Kung Peninsula★
清水灣與西貢

From Diamond Hill or Choi Hung MTR, take bus no. 92 to the end of the line.

Seafood lovers make a beeline for Sai Kung, though the peninsula is not easily accessible. You'll have to take the MTR and then the bus, which means more than an hour to get there. Your efforts, however, will be richly rewarded.

Clear Water Bay Country Park
清水灣郊野公園
On Clear Water Bay Rd.

The first area you come to on the east shore, this scenic park bordered by rocky cliffs is a great place for hiking. The 6.6km/4mi **High Junk Peak Country Trail** – popular with both hikers and mountain bikers – follows the contours of the peninsula's ridge and skirts High Junk Peak, the park's loftiest at 344m/1,128ft. Fine views of the bay abound along the trip, as the trail winds its way down to Joss House Bay, the location of **Tin Hau Temple★★★** *(see Temples)*. If you prefer a more relaxing outdoor experience, head for one of the park's two sandy guarded

---

New Territories, Old Ways

Despite their 21C leanings, the New Territories present vestiges of their early days to those who know where to look. This area was first settled primarily by the Hakka ethnic group, once known as the gypsies of China. Living primarily in the barren eastern parts of the New Territories in the late 17C, the Hakka fished, farmed and quarried stone to make their living. Today, despite having mingled with Hong Kong's gene pool, the Hakka community remains visible in some rural pockets. You will still see some older women wearing traditional dark blue or black tunic tops and pants, and wide-brimmed bamboo hats fringed with cloth. Most of the younger generation, however, gave up the rustic life long ago and relocated to be closer to their city workplaces. In the central and west New Territories, Hong Kong's surviving monasteries are maintained by monks and nuns who have not succumbed to the territory's famously materialistic mindset.

Kowloon to Canton Railway (KCR) trains run up the center of the New Territories, and the MTR quickly connects to Tsuen Wan in the west, where the tram-like Light Rail Transit (LRT) carriages service Tsuen Mun. For the eastern part of the New Territories there is no rail; bus and minibus services are the way to go – or splurge on a taxi. All public roads, like everywhere in Hong Kong, are in good condition. While the same is true for hiking trails – mostly paved paths – do not attempt remote hikes in potentially rainy weather, as streams can flood paths and mudslides occasionally occur. And do take a hat, plenty of water, and sunscreen.

beaches, which attract families on weekends with on-site parking, changing and showering facilities, and barbecue pits.

Sai Kung Town 西貢市
On Clear Water Bay Rd.
Farther on, past the exclusive pleasure-boat-filled mooring at Marina Cove, is Sai Kung Town and the terminus for the buses. Surrounded by hills sprinkled with Spanish-style villas, Sai Kung feels like a cross between a Chinese fishing village and a Mediterranean port. A promenade lined with tanks of live fish and sprinkled with the outdoor tables of seafood restaurants overlooks a harbor full of fishing boats.

To see the harbor from a different perspective, take a ride on a **sampan** – a small wooden fishing boat. Operators openly solicit business and expect a bit of haggling from potential passengers; fares start at around HK$80 for a tour of the harbor. Fishermen sell their catch from boats at various times of day. Plenty of open-fronted restaurants offer European cuisine, reflecting a significant Caucasian residential community here.

Nearby is the **Pak Tam Chung Nature Trail**, and on it the tiny **Sheung Yiu Folk Museum** *(from Sai Kung, take bus no. 94; open Wed–Mon 9am–4pm except public holidays; 2792 6365; www.heritagemuseum.gov.hk).* Formerly a fortified village, the museum displays the traditional way of life of the Hakka people, who once lived here (see sidebar, p67).

Sha Tin★ 沙田
Less than 13km/8mi north of Tsim Sha Tsui, the village of Sha Tin used to be surrounded by fields that produced a delicious type of pomelo, a pale green citrus fruit. When you step out of the MTR station, though, don't expect to see a rural setting.

Fishing Boats, Sai Kung Town

Hong Kong Tourism Board

REGIONS

55

Some 700,000 people live in Sha Tin New Town today and, sadly, nothing is left of its rural village atmosphere. **Sha Tin Racecourse** (see Horse Racing), the **Hong Kong Heritage Museum**★★ (see Cultural Museums) and meditative spots like the the **Ten Thousand Buddhas Monastery**★ and **Che King Temple** (see Temples) are the reasons most people come here.

New Kowloon 新九龍

Located past Boundary Street (which marked the border with China when the New Territories were not yet part of the colony), these areas are not officially part of Kowloon. However, urban development has integrated them little by little into the tip of the peninsula – so much so that they are often described under the name "New Kowloon."

Jockey Club Creative Arts Centre★
賽馬會創意藝術中心
30 Pak Tin St., Shek Kip Mei. MTR: Shek Kip Mei (head up Woh Chai St., then go right on Pak Tin St. and continue until you come to a large green building). Open year- *round daily 10am–10pm. Guided tour in English (40min) at 4pm. 2353 1311. www.jccac.org.hk.*

For many years, Shek Kip Mei was synonymous with a terrible 1953 fire that devastated the makeshift shelters that once crowded this site, leaving 50,000 Chinese homeless refugees. To give them a place to live, the governor built countless multicolored buildings equipped with fire- and flood-resistant devices. The bright exterior colors don't at all reflect the sad reality of the conditions inside the apartments: five people per 28m²/301sq ft, rented for HK$14 per month.

Even so, Hong Kong residents consider this to be part of their history, and have opposed several attempts at renovation.

Among the buildings that make up the compound, a **former factory** became a center for the arts in 2008.

This energetic collection of small visual, music and literary studios is spread over several floors arranged around an interior central courtyard; more than 150 artists rent out space at the Centre. G.O.D. (Goods of Desire), a local brand

Cattle Village Art Depot

© Tao Images/Photoshot

Tai Mo Shan

© Ulana Switucha/Alamy

specializing in updated Asian products (*see Shopping*) has a branch here.

Cattle Village Art Depot
牛棚藝術村
63 Ma Tau Kok Rd., To Kwan Wan. MTR: Mong Kok or Yau Ma Tei; then take a taxi. Open year-round Tue–Sun 2pm–8pm. 2104 3322.
This former slaughterhouse in Kowloon City was converted by the government into a modern art center in 2001. Artists can rent a workspace for a pittance during their first year here.
You can roam around the complex and tour the galleries, workshops and theaters, which represent many attempts to spark Hong Kong's creative juices.

Tsuen Wan 荃灣

MTR: Tsuen Wan.

If you have extra time in Hong Kong, Tsuen Wan offers a perfect opportunity to leave the beaten path. The town is the starting point for five nature trails in the New Territories – the Maclehose being the longest at around 100km/62mi.

Sam Tung Uk Museum
棟屋博物館
2 Kwu Uk Lane. MTR: Tsuen Wan and follow signs from the station. Open Wed–Mon 9am–5pm; closed holidays. 2411 2001. www.lcsd. gov.hk/stum.
A 17C fortified village built by an agrarian clan of Hakkas from the province of Fujian, Sam Tunk Uk preserves the history of this former village. With the major urban development of Tsuen Wan, villagers deserted the place, and in 1981, the site was declared a museum. Restored to its original appearance, all Sam Tung Uk lacks is the bustling atmosphere of a lived-in village.

Tai Mo Shan 大帽山
From Tsuen Wan, bus 51 departing from Nina Tower 1.
Tai Mo Shan, or "Big Hat Mountain," overlooks Hong Kong. Scaling it takes about six hours. If you plan to try it, don't forget your gear: hiking map, food and water, and a good pair of boots. The panoramic view from the peak, if the weather is clear, will more than justify the efforts you made to get to the top.

THEME TOURS

There are many ways to see Hong Kong, but to get a good overview, we suggest the following thematic itineraries. Sites in bold can be found in the Index.

⚓ Star Ferry 天星小輪

For ferry details, see Family Fun.
Essential to any visit to Hong Kong, a ride in the Star Ferry that runs between Tsim Sha Tsui and Central is a must-do. The green and white ferries have been plying Victoria Harbour for more than a century. From the Star Ferry Pier in Central, the boats – which all have "Star" in their names – take commuters to Tsim Sha Sui in about eight minutes. Snag a seat on the top level for the best views. Other ferries departing from Central will take you to the **Outlying Islands** (*see Excursions*).

Markets 市場

For the best market tour, you can't beat the **Mong Kok** neighborhood. Visit the markets on the north part of Hong Kong Island early in the morning, when the electronic shops are just opening one by one, and end your day at the Temple Street Night Market. The **Flower Market**, next to the Jordan MTR station, is where you'll find gorgeous orchids and exotic plants. Just a few steps away is the **Bird Market★★**.

You can purchase a cage here, but beware that some of them are quite expensive. Leave the birds for the **Goldfish Market**, which sells another pet preferred by the Chinese – one that is said to bring good fortune.

The **Ladies Market** hawks modern wares, such as CDs, luggage and – despite its name – clothing for both women and men. Next to the **Tin Hau Temple★★★**, the **Jade Market★** sells a wide range of items made out of the green semi-precious stone. At night, Temple Street closes to traffic, and you can roam through the chaos of vendors and search for souvenirs in the **Temple Street Night Market★★★** (*see Street Markets*).

Bird Market, Mong Kok

Florent Bonnefoy/Michelin

GIFT RECEIPT

Barnes & Noble Booksellers #2318
910 Highland Colony Pkwy #3009

Ridgeland, MS 39157
(601) 605-4028

STR:2318 REG:008 TRN:8883 CSHR:Michelle M

Michelin Must Sees Hong Kong
  9781907099434   T1
  (1 @ RV.HH)   RV.HH G

Thanks for shopping at
Barnes & Noble

101.28A   09/09/2012 02:03PM

CUSTOMER COPY

a gift receipt is presented within 60 days of purchase; (iii) for textbooks, or (iv) for products purchased at Barnes & Noble College bookstores that are listed for sale in the Barnes & Noble Booksellers inventory management system.

Opened music CDs/DVDs/audio books may not be returned, and can be exchanged only for the same title and only if defective. NOOKs purchased from other retailers or sellers are returnable only to the retailer or seller from which they are purchased, pursuant to such retailer's or seller's return policy. Magazines, newspapers, eBooks, digital downloads, and used books are not returnable or exchangeable. Defective NOOKs may be exchanged at the store in accordance with the applicable warranty.

Returns or exchanges will not be permitted (i) after 14 days or without receipt or (ii) for product not carried by Barnes & Noble or Barnes & Noble.com.

Policy on receipt may appear in two sections.

Return Policy

<u>With a sales receipt or Barnes & Noble.com packing slip</u>, a full refund in the original form of payment will be issued from any Barnes & Noble Booksellers store for returns of undamaged NOOKs, new and unread books, and unopened and undamaged music CDs, DVDs, and audio books made within 14 days of purchase from a Barnes & Noble Booksellers store or Barnes & Noble.com with the below exceptions:

A store credit for the purchase price will be issued (i) for purchases

Hong Kong in the Movies

Long a center for the film industry in Asia, Hong Kong has produced a number of movie stars whose fame knows no borders. The three actors below have all been honored on the Hong Kong **Avenue of Stars★**.

Maggie Cheung, the first Asian actress to win an award at the Cannes Film Festival in France, has starred in over 80 films and received 8 international awards since her career launched in 1983. Martial arts master **Bruce Lee** moved to the US at age 18. His role in films like *The Big Boss* (1971), *Way of the Dragon* (1972) and *The Game of Death* (1978), sparked an interest in Chinese martial arts in the West.

Avenue of Stars

© winhorse/iStockphoto.com

Known for his acrobatic fighting style and comic genius, **Jackie Chan** cut his cinematic teeth in Hong Kong in 1979 with Yen Woo Ping's film *Drunken Master*. Chan also claims a star on the Hollywood Walk of Fame in Los Angeles, California.

🚊 Tram Tour 叮叮車

For tram details, see Family Fun.
While the tram is not the fastest way to discover Hong Kong, it is one of the cheapest. Trams circulate between Shau Kei Wan and Kennedy town, with one line going out to Happy Valley.
Start from Causeway Bay, where you can take an early walk in Victoria Park. The tram will take you through Wan Chai and Admiralty; step off here if you want to walk to **Saint John's Cathedral★** or **Hong Kong Park★★**.
If you get back on the tram, you will pass Central's skyscrapers and **Statue Square★**. Continue your tour in Central, where you can shop and grab a bite to eat; or visit the **Zoological and Botanical Gardens★**, a stone's throw away from the **Government House**. The tram then continues west to **Sheung Wan★★★**, last stop on this

tour, known for the shops around **Bonham Strand★★**, which stock all the pharmacopeia related to traditional Chinese medicine.

🐾 Walking Tour of the Mid-Levels 半山區步行

One of the best ways to discover Sheung Wan and the **Mid-Levels★★★** is to walk. Start at the Mid-Levels escalators and step off at **Hollywood Road★★**. Walk down this road lined with antique shops to the **Man Mo Temple★★★** and upper Lascar Row – better known as **Cat Street**.
On the escalators (*entrance on Robinson Rd.*) you can cross Hollywood Road and climb higher into the Mid-Levels. Along the way, you'll cross Staunton Road, location of myriad bars and restaurants. From there, you can proceed to Caine Road, location of the **Dr. Sun Yat-sen Museum**.

THEME TOURS

59

SKYSCRAPERS

You see them on most Hong Kong guidebook covers, postcards, calendars, T-shirts and other souvenirs. The territory's towering skyscrapers are indeed a significant and inspiring part of the urban landscape. The skyscrapers that most visitors see are the more prominent ones in Central, owned by banks or Hong Kong's handful of major property developers, who can afford the fees of big-name international architects. Move away from the business districts of Central and you'll find newer, more functional and less aesthetic office and residential towers that blot out the sunlight in West Kowloon. The new **LegCo Tower** in Admiralty, where government lawmakers will debate politics, is scheduled for completion in fall 2011. The finished structure will take the shape of an open doorway, symbolizing transparency within government.

Bank of China Tower★★
中銀大廈

1 Garden Rd., Central.
MTR: Central.

Famed Chinese architect I.M. Pei (who designed the Louvre pyramid in Paris) conceived this 367m/1,205ft skyscraper in the shape of a sprouting bamboo shoot; each section of the 70-story structure corresponds to the parts of a bamboo stalk, representing new growth and the rapid development of the Bank of China. Completed in 1989 and sheathed

in dark glass panels, this compilation of four triangular shafts is fervently disparaged by feng shui practitioners. They claim the tower resembles a butcher knife with its cutting edge turned toward HSBC, suggesting cutthroat competition between the two institutions. Knife or not, Bank of China Tower is now the fourth-highest structure in Hong Kong. A small **observation deck** (*open during office hours; closed weekends; passport or ID required for entrance*) on the 43rd floor of the building is open to the public.

HSBC Tower★★
香港滙豐總行大廈

1 Queen's Rd., Central.
MTR: Central.

Piercing the Central skyline, HSBC Tower is one of the city's most recognizable buildings. When British architect Sir Norman Foster took on the task of designing the headquarters of the former Hongkong & Shanghai Banking Corporation, he faced the challenge of fitting the massive structure that the bank envisioned

Bank of China Tower

Florent Bonnefoy/Michelin

MUST SEE

into a relatively small space where the former bank building had stood. His solution to this problem was to eliminate the central core. The tower's framework thus hangs from five giant trusses, supported by eight groups of aluminum-wrapped steel pillars that bear the weight of the 180m/590ft-tall building. This audacious project proved the most expensive construction at the time – using some 30,000 tons of steel, 4,500 tons of aluminum, and racking up a cost of over a billion US dollars. Natural light pours into the 10-story atrium, courtesy of computer-controlled mirrors that reflect sunlight down into the public plaza below. From this space, two escalators lead up to the main banking hall. They were designed according to the principles of **feng shui** (*see SIDEBAR, above*), to funnel the flow of *qi* into the offices above. At the entrance, the two bronze lions that guard the bank's doors are survivors of the former building and WWII.

International Commerce Centre
環球貿易廣場

1 Austin Rd., West Kowloon. MTR: Central.

Imposing at 484m/1,587ft, the International Commerce Centre (ICC; built 2010) ranks as the tallest building in Hong Kong. It houses the Ritz-Carlton (*see Hotels*) and **Sky 100** (*see Regions/Kowloon*), the highest indoor observation deck in the city. Apart from a few restaurants on its upper floors, the building is occupied by finance companies.

Along with 90-story **Two International Finance Centre** (built 2003), designed by re-nowned architect Cesar Pelli, these two office towers reign as the tallest in the city.

Both Two IFC and ICC are located near the waterfront, but the former stands in Hong Kong's Central District. From the air or the water, the two piles visually suggest a gateway to Victoria Harbour.

TEMPLES

Although the island's skyscrapers are what first greet the eye, and a plethora of glitzy malls displaying the wares of top international designers might give the impression of a Westernized slice of China, there are vestiges of the old ways here in Hong Kong's many temples. Hundreds of temples, shrines and monasteries are scattered throughout the territory, where people of all ages come to pay their respects to their preferred Buddhist and Taoist deities. During lunar calendar festivals, most temples overflow with visitors bringing offerings, donating money and having their fortunes told.

Chi Lin Nunnery★★★
志蓮淨苑

5 Chi Lin Dr., Diamond Hill, New Territories. MTR: Diamond Hill. Open year-round daily 7am–9pm. 2354 1888. www.chilin.org.hk. See Chinese Heritage Sites.

🔥 Man Mo Temple★★★
文武廟

126 Hollywood Rd., Mid-Levels, Hong Kong Island. MTR: Sheung Wan. 2540 0350. Open daily 8am–6pm.

This small but very popular temple, nestled in a curve of Hollywood Road, dates to before the colonial period. It is surrounded by a spiritual fervor made even more bewitching by the clouds of incense that hang in the air here. Look up and you'll see the source: giant incense coils, which can burn as long as three weeks, hang from the ceiling inside the temple. Their aromatic smoke carries prayers to the spirit world.

Man Mo is home to two divinities: Man Cheong and Kuan Ti, both of whom are represented by statues brought from mainland China. The first, clad in red robes and holding a calligraphy brush, protects civil servants. The second, dressed in green and wielding a sword, depicts General Guan Yu of the Three Kingdoms period in his divine form. The temple, one of the oldest in Hong Kong, built in 1840, honors literature (*man*) and

Incense Coils, Man Mo Temple

Florent Bonnefoy/Michelin

Wishing Trees

From Taipo Market train station, take bus no. 64K, 65K or minibus 25K.

If you're in town during the Chinese New Year celebration, do as the locals do and make a pilgrimage to the Lam Tseun wishing trees, two banyan trees that were planted during the Qing Dynasty (1644-1912). Located near Tin Hau Temple, the two trees each represent different types of wishes; the big tree relates to education, business, wealth and good health, while the smaller one covers marriage and children.

It's a local Taoist tradition to come here and write your name, birth date and wishes on a piece of brightly colored joss paper, roll the paper up, tie it to an orange, and toss it up into one of the trees. As legend has it, the higher you can place your wish on the tree, the more likely it is to come true. In recent years, the practice of tying wishes to the trees has been banned. Now wooden racks beside the banyans serve as receptacles for the paper wishes.

the military (*mo*). Notice the case displaying markers, pencils and pens. These are objects blessed by Man Cheong, which students often purchase as good-luck charms for their studies.

Tin Hau Temple★★★
天后廟

Yue Shau Tau Square, Yau Ma Tei, Kowloon. MTR: Yau Ma Tei. Open daily 8am–6pm.

Set in the heart of Yau Ma Tei, Tin Hau Temple fronts a square bordered by giant banyan trees, where the locals gather in the shade to play Mahjong and backgammon. Dating from 1876, the building is one of the oldest in Hong Kong. The temple has been renovated several times over the years, and though the present bunker-style exterior is unimpressive – the temple's roof tiles are painted green to repel bad spirits – the interior retains its traditional look.

Tin Hau is the protector of fishermen – a reminder that Yau Ma Tei used to be a bay, where the Tanka people lived in boats. The sea here has been pushed back little by little over the years by land reclamation all over Hong Kong, so Tin Hau Temple today no longer borders the waterfront.

Three other temples have been added to the main building. On the left is the temple of Shea Tan, dedicated to the protector of the local community; and on the right is that of Shing Wong, the protector of the city, who is believed to report the good and bad deeds of each individual to the heavenly gods. The third is Fook Tak, where To Tei (god of the soil) and Kwan Yin (goddess of mercy) are worshipped.

Tin Hau presides over the main hall from an elevated platform behind the altar. On the right side of the altar, note the guardian divinities of each year in a cycle of 60 years of the Chinese lunar calendar; try

Touring Tip

When visiting temples in Hong Kong, it is appropriate to leave a small donation before you depart.

TEMPLES

A Chinese Pantheon

To maintain order in a world of chaos, the Chinese worship many gods and goddesses – each possessing unique abilities. The Chinese believe that these deities have dominion over every part of life; there is a god of the harvest, a god of the wind, a god who protects travelers, a god of students, and even a god of the bedroom. Among the most popular gods in Hong Kong, **Tin Hau**, the Queen of Heaven, is a deification of the daughter of a government official who lived in the Fujian Province in the tenth century. She is said to have rescued a group of fishermen during a storm, and when she died, the local villagers built a temple to honor her. Today Tin Hau is worshipped as the goddess of the sea.

Kwan Yin, the goddess of mercy and compassion, is a manifestation of the Divine Mother, while **Wong Tai Sin**, a shepherd born around A.D. 328, is believed to be able to cure sickness. The Man Mo Temple honors **Man**, the god of literature, and **Mo**, the god of war – ironically the patron of both the Triads (organized gangs) and the police.

to spot the god that protects your birth year.

In the evening, **fortune tellers** and feng shui masters hold consultations outdoors on the temple grounds – and some of them speak English. The **Temple Street Night Market★★★** (see *Street Markets*) is only a few blocks away from the temple, heading east down Kansu Road.

Tin Hau Temple

Florent Bonnefoy/Michelin

Wong Tai Sin Temple★★★ 黃大仙祠

2 Chuk Yuen Village, Wong Tai Sin, New Territories. Open daily 7am–5:30pm. MTR: Wong Tai Sin.

This ornate temple shows off the traditional Chinese style in its two-tiered golden roof, bright red pillars, blue friezes and yellow latticework. Set in compact but beautifully landscaped grounds, Wong Tai Sin was rebuilt in 1973 in the late 19C Qing dynasty style. It is home to the healing Taoist god Wong Tai Sin. A portrait of him as a young shepherd, which hangs in the main temple, was brought from Mainland China in 1915. The reason many come to this site is to determine their fortunes. Wong Tai Sin also possesses the virtue of spreading **good fortune**, so some gamblers come here before heading out to the casinos and racecourses. They burn incense and paper offerings, and obtain calendars to help choose the most auspicious day for betting. Fortune tellers, who set up

Ten Thousand Buddhas Monastery

© Ella/Fotolia.com

in the arcade by the entrance, will read your palm, your face or even your feet.

As you approach the main room, stop and listen. You will hear what sounds like a drum roll; this sound is made by sticks being stirred in dozens of bamboo pots by those who seeking answers to their questions (*see sidebar, p50*).

Ten Thousand Buddhas Monastery★ 萬佛寺

Sha Tin, New Territories. MTR: Sha Tin (follow the signs from train station; it's a 20min walk or a 5min taxi ride). MTR: Sha Tin. Open daily 9am–5pm. 2691 1067.

This complex of small prayer halls is an absolute highlight of Hong Kong's cultural heritage, a few minutes from the bustle of Sha Tin town. You have to climb more than 400 winding steps – lined with 500 gold statues of Buddha's disciples – to reach this monastery.

In the main hall, you'll find a dizzying array of Buddha statuettes – 13,000 of them, in fact, and no two are exactly alike. Here too,

lies the embalmed and gold-leaf-covered body of Yuet Kai, the monk who founded the temple. Outside in the temple courtyard, note the nine-story pink pagoda.

Che Kung Temple 車公廟

7 Che Kung Temple Rd., New Territories. MTR: Tai Wai. Open daily 7am–6pm.

A few minutes' walk from the MTR station, this Taoist temple complex honors Che Kung, a general from the Sung Dynasty (A.D. 960–1279) who quashed a rebellion in South China and reportedly rid Guangdong province of a fatal plague. The site always hums with devotees in attendance, making offerings and uttering prayers. During the lunar New Year, visitors have to line up to spin the fan-bladed metal wheels of fortune (they look like and are about the same size as children's windmills) that line the courtyard. Worshippers believe that these wheels bring good luck when turned three times.

CHINESE HERITAGE SITES

Sights in this section preserve some of the rich Chinese heritage that abounds in Hong Kong, alongside the trappings of the modern city. From a tranquil convent to an abandoned walled city to trails that lead past ancient temples and forgotten villages, it's worth spending time to discover the region's fascinating past.

Chi Lin Nunnery★★★
志蓮淨苑

5 Chi Lin Dr., Diamond Hill, New Territories. MTR: Diamond Hill. Open year-round daily 7am–9pm. 2354 1888. www.chilin.org.hk.

In contrast to the noisy and colorful Wong Tai Sin Temple, the Chi Lin Nunnery is serene and restrained. The complex, where a few nuns still live, was built in 1930. The sanctuary and garden, renovated in 1990 to the tune of some HK$90 million, is a revival of the Tang dynasty (618-907) style, borrowed from the Japanese and still used today. The Main Hall was built without nails, using a system of interlocking sections of wood. This is the place to go for tranquil meditation. Lotus flowers float on the ponds, and with a little luck, the bougainvillea will be in bloom, adding its bright fuchsia hue to the landscape. Inside, large statues of Buddha and bodhisattvas await worshippers. A bronze bell is meant to appease the soul's suffering when it sounds. An outdoor continuation of the temple, **Nan Lian Garden** (*see Parks and Gardens*) abounds with pools, waterfalls and bridges – and a golden pavilion rising from a pond framed by pine trees. The serenity of the place is only disturbed by the chirping of birds and the conversations of passersby. A teahouse, beside one of the ponds, and a vegetarian restaurant, sitting under a waterfall, offer refreshment to those who wish to linger.

Wong Tai Sin Temple★★★ 黃大仙祠

2 Chuk Yuen Village, Wong Tai Sin, New Territories. Open year-round daily 7am–5:30pm. MTR: Wong Tai Sin. See Temples.

Ten Thousand Buddhas Monastery★ 萬佛寺

Sha Tin, New Territories. MTR: Sha Tin (follow the signs from train station; it's a 20min walk or a 5min taxi ride). Open daily 9am–5pm. 2691 1067. See Temples.

Chi Lin Nunnery

Florent Bonnefoy/Michelin

Sheung Yiu Folk Museum

On Pak Tam Chung Nature Trail, Sai Kung, New Territories. From Sai Kung, take bus 94. Open year-round Wed–Mon 9am–4pm. Closed public holidays. 2792 6365. www.heritagemuseum.gov.hk. If you'd like to discover the traditional way of life of the Hakka people who once lived on the peninsula, visit this little museum, located at one of the entrances to scenic **Sai Kung Country Park**. The museum, which occupies an area of 500m²/5,382sq ft, encompasses a fortified village built in the late 19C. The village and its neighboring limestone kiln were declared protected monuments in 1981. After a painstaking restoration, the site opened as a museum in 1984.

Kowloon Walled City Park 九龍寨城公園

Tung Tau Tsuen Rd., Kowloon City, New Territories. MTR: Lok Fu (then take a taxi). Open year-round daily 6:30am–11pm. 2716 9962. www.lcsd.gov.hk.

The site of a Chinese fort, built in 1847 to protect Kowloon's shoreline, this once-infamous neighborhood now sparkles as one of the region's best parks. After the colonization of the New Territories, the Chinese managed to maintain control of the zone through a legal loophole. The garrison set up in the walled village eventually became a self-sufficient community. At the end of WWII, the British should have been able to recuperate the jurisdiction, but they didn't count on the massive surge of Chinese refugees to the area. Kowloon Walled City became a no-man's land, frequented by the Triads (Chinese crime gangs). In the 1980s, the stronghold developed a reputation for brothels, casinos, opium dens, and other illegal activities; and the population, which had risen to 30,000 by that time, lived in complete anarchy. After the Sino-British Joint Declaration, the two governments decided that this situation could not continue. In 1987, an agreement was signed to destroy the seedy district and re-house its 50,000 inhabitants. A lovely park was built on the ruins, in the style of classic **Jiangnan gardens** (in the fashion of Suzhou, located near Shanghai on the Mainland), where the poetic names of the pavilions and copses of rare trees belie the site's shady past. The only souvenirs of the town's early days are kept in the *yamen* (the office and residence of the administrator of Kowloon under the Qing Dynasty) as a photographic exhibition of the former citadel.

© Leung Cho Pan/Dreamstime.com

Kowloon Walled City Park

Lung Yeuk Tau Heritage Trail 龍躍頭文物徑

Fanling, New Territories. MTR: Fanling (from the station take green minibus 54K or a taxi to Lung Yeuk Tau and get off at the village of Shung Him Tong (then follow signs). www.lcsd.gov.hk.

Northeast of Luen Wo Hui in Fanling, this heritage trail passes several historic structures of Lung Yeuk Tau, otherwise known as either Lung Ku Tau, or Lung Ling (Mountain of the Dragon) for the leaping dragon of local legend that once supposedly lived in the area. The Tangs here rank as one of the Five Great Clans of the New Territories, originating from Jiangxi province in Mainland China. They have a noble descent that traces back to the eldest son of a princess of the Southern Song dynasty (1127-1279), who took refuge in South China and married a member of the Tang clan. Her eldest son moved to Lung Yeuk Tau, where the clan built five walled villages and six non-walled ones in the area; the trail passes through six of them. Some structures date back to the 18C

and several to the 19C. Today the Tangs still practice traditional village customs including the communal worship in spring and autumn, and a lantern-lighting ceremony for newborn boys on the 15th day of the first Lunar month. Well-maintained traditional Chinese buildings include the Tang Chung Ling Ancestral Hall and the Tin Hau Kung temple (devoted to Tin Hau, the goddess of the sea). Notice also the residences in some of the walled villages, such as Lo Wai and San Wan, which retain their historic appearance.

Ping Shan Heritage Trail 屏山文物徑

Tin Shui Wai, Yuen Long, New Territories. MTR: Tin Shui Wai. www.lcsd.gov.hk.

The district of Ping Shan is distinguished from others in Hong Kong by its long history, involving another line of the Tang clan, which has lived in the area since the 12C. Take a half-day excursion to explore the numerous structures that still stand here from that era and tell the story of the historical

Lung Yeuk Tau Heritage Trail

© Alex Havret/Apa Publications

MUST SEE

and social developments that have taken place over the centuries. Stretching about 1km/0.6mi in length, the Ping Shan Heritage Trail meanders through the villages of Hang Mei Tsuen, Hang Tau Tsuen and Sheung Cheung Wai. Buildings lie easy walking distance from each other and give a good insight into traditional life in the New Territories.

Unique monuments on the trail include Hong Kong's only ancient pagoda – the hexagonal **Tsui Sing Lau Pagoda** (a.k.a. the Pagoda of Gathering Stars) – and the **Tang Ancestral Hall**, one of the largest in the territory.

Other highlights are **Sheung Cheung Wai** walled village and **Kun Ting Study Hall** – built for high school and college students. Keep an eye out for some of the well-preserved temples too. Informative signposts are posted along the trail.

Sam Tung Uk Museum
棟屋博物館

2 Kwu Uk Lane, Tsuen Wan, New Territories. MTR: Tsuen Wan (follow signs from the subway station). Open year-round Wed–Mon 9am–5pm. Closed holidays. 2411 2001. www.lcsd.gov.hk. ***See Regions/New Territories.***

This fortified 17C village built by an agrarian clan of the Hakka people merits a visit if you have extra time in Hong Kong.

Tai Fu Tai Mansion
大夫第

Tai Fu Tai Mansion

Hong Kong Tourism Board

San Tin Village, Sheung Shui, New Territories. MTR: Sheung Shui. From the station, take bus 76K to San Tin near the post office, and follow the signs; it's a 10min walk to the museum. Open year-round Wed–Mon 9am–1pm & 2pm–5pm.

This elegant house with its interior courtyard was built as a residence in 1865, during the Qing Dynasty, by scholar Man Chung-luen of the Man clan in San Tun. The mansion, restored in 1988, is considered one of the most beautifully embellished traditional Chinese structures in Hong Kong. It is famed for its fine exterior and interior adornments – even though its windowless façade resembles a fortress. Doors and roof eaves are decoratively painted. In the hall of ancestors, note the photographs of deceased members of the Man clan that hang on the wall.

Within its well-tended gardens sits **Man Tin-cheung Memorial Park**, marked by a statue honoring Man Tin-cheung (1236-1282) – a poet and the last prime minister of the Sung dynasty, who was executed by the Mongols following a three-year imprisonment.

COLONIAL SITES

Not many of Hong Kong's colonial 19th- or even early 20th-century structures avoided the demolition ball during the city's rampant transition from a scattering of fishing villages to its skyscraper-studded modern landscape. Apart from the structures listed below, all that remains of the colonial days are vintage photographic records of the grand arcaded buildings that used locally quarried granite and other stone, and the lifestyle that disappeared along with them. You'll have to be satisfied with a glimpse of the former **French Mission Building**, built on Battery Path in Central in 1917 (not open for public tours). Inside Flagstaff House, a preserved c.1840s mansion that can be visited, you'll find the **Museum of Teaware**★★★ *(see Cultural Museums)*. In SoHo, the **Fringe Club** *(see Performing Arts)* and the adjoining Foreign Correspondents Club provide examples of the red-brick and cream-colored-stone façades of Hong Kong's early 20C structures.

Saint John's Cathedral★
聖約翰座堂

4-8 Garden Rd., Central. MTR: Central. Open year-round 9am–5pm, Sat & Sun 9am–noon. 2523 4157. www.stjohnscathedral. org.hk.

Dwarfed by the shadows of Central's surrounding skyscrapers, the oldest Anglican church in the Far East was consecrated in 1847. The cathedral, with its cream-colored façade and harmonious proportions, is a fine example of colonial Hong Kong architecture. Notice the ceiling in the shape of a boat's hull, from which large

Saint John's Cathedral

Hong Kong Tourism Board

Government House

Peer through the gates of Government House (*Upper Albert Rd.; not open to the public; MTR: Central*) for a glance at the place where the current and many previous heads of Hong Kong work. The 1855 colonial mansion is the official residence of Hong Kong's political premiere, Chief Executive Donald Tsang. There are ceaseless debates on its *feng shui* configuration; the threatening shape of the nearby Bank of China Tower is said to be pointing toward the former colonial government seat. To protect himself from negative forces, Tsang reportedly keeps a pond of carp in the garden grounds in order to radiate positive energy.

ceiling fans hang to cool the congregation. Towards the choir, lovely stained-glass windows illustrate passages from the Bible and scenes from life in the former colony.

Legislative Council (LegCo) Building
香港立法會

Queen's Rd., Central. MTR: Central.

The LegCo Building on **Statue Square★** is where the Hong Kong Government has voted in its laws since the early 1970s. And what better place to do it than in the 1912 Supreme Court Building, which housed the court until 1985. Look up to see LegCo's iconic feature, the 2.7m/9ft-tall statue of Themis – the blindfolded Greek Goddess of Justice – which crowns the building's central pediment. In fall 2011, this building will return to is judicial roots, becoming the Court of Final Appeal.

Murray House 美利樓

On Stanley Main Rd., Stanley, Hong Kong Island. Stanley Buses 6, 6A, 6X and 260 from Exchange Square.

Now set on the edge of the bay, this building stood for a century and a half in Central – at the spot now occupied by the Bank of China Tower – until 1982, when it was dismantled, the granite blocks numbered (the numbers are still visible if you look closely) and put into storage. It was only recently (1998) that the house was reassembled here.
One of the earliest colonial structures in Hong Kong, Murray House dates to 1843, when it was used as a mess hall for British army

Stanley War Cemetery

Stanley Main St., Stanley.
On the well-kept grounds of Stanley War Cemetery, you can trace the earliest colonial days through the gravestones of foreign and local military personnel and their families. The number of fatalities due to disease, particularly of young children and babies, is surprising. But the dominant stones mark the often untimely deaths of British and Commonwealth servicemen, who met their end when Hong Kong fell on Christmas Day in 1941 to Japanese troops – some of them living out their last miserable days as prisoners of war. Survey the memorial stones, where parts of the attempt to defend the then-British territory are chronicled.

officers. Inside are some smart but reasonably priced restaurants where you can enjoy international cuisine and waterfront views.

Hong Kong Tourism Board

Murray House

CULTURAL MUSEUMS

One thing Hong Kong has plenty of is museums. In the past decade or so, two of the best, the **Hong Kong Museum of History★★★** and the **Hong Kong Science Museum** *(see Family Fun)* – were revamped to become high-tech and interactive. The former remains a great place to get an insight into the territory's past and present.

Glean a briefer point of reference for Hong Kong's modern history at the small but informative galleries at the **Sky 100** observation deck *(see Regions/Kowloon)*.

One of the territory's few heritage museums, **Sheung Yiu Folk Museum** *(see Chinese Heritage Sites)* sits along leafy Pak nature trail in Sai Kung. This small village is presented as it might have looked more than a century ago.

Hong Kong Museum of Art★★★
香港藝術館

10 Salisbury Rd., Tsim Sha Tsui, Kowloon. MTR: Tsim Sha Tsui. Open year-round Fri–Wed 10am–6pm (Sat until 8pm). Closed Thu & holidays. HK$10. 2721 0116. www.hk.art.museum.

The Hong Kong Museum of Art is an important stop for anyone interested in Chinese culture, and especially that of Southern China. The museum's collections number more than 15,700 objects, including antique treasures as well as works by local artists. Highlights of the collection are displayed in exhibition galleries on four floors. The **gallery of Chinese antiques**, spread out over the first and third floors, includes superb ceramics, Shiwan pottery – renowned for its fisherman motif – and finely glazed porcelain. **Song Dynasty pieces★★** (960-1279), rendered in what is called the Jun style, are remarkable for the lovely celadon glaze that gives them a soft blue appearance. Notice also the imposing ceramic **statue of Buddha★** dating from 1617. Buddha is represented seated on a lotus and his tunic is covered with blue enamels.

In the **Xubaizhai Gallery of Chinese Painting and Calligraphy★** *(second floor)* you will find a great number of silk scrolls (some longer than 4m/13ft). A small **calligraphy collection★** includes two originals of the reformists Liang Qichao (1873-1929) and Kang Youwei (1858-1927), interesting for their historical value. The collection also contains an ancient copy of *Preface to the Poems Composed at the Orchid Pavilion*, executed by one of the Chinese masters of calligraphy,

Song Dynasty Bowl, Hong Kong Museum of Art

Florent Bonnefoy/Michelin

Wang Xi Zhi (303-361). Lovers of old Hong Kong will enjoy the section of photos and lithographs depicting Hong Kong, Macau and Canton during the colonial days. On the second floor, the special exhibition gallery holds temporary shows of modern Hong Kong art; in recent years, some cutting-edge video and installation pieces have appeared here.

♨ Hong Kong Museum of History★★★
香港歷史博物館

100 Chatham Road South, Tsim Sha Tsui, Kowloon. MTR: Tsim Sha Tsui. Open year-round Fri–Wed 10am–6pm. Closed holidays. HK$10. 2724 9042. www.hk. history.museum.

Touring Tip

Families with children, fear not: the Hong Kong Museum of History has plenty of exhibits to hold the interest of little ones. The Neolithic and Wildlife of Hong Kong galleries have great appeal for kids. Models of prehistoric creatures and dioramas of the earliest human fishing communities pique their interest too. Check out the re-created village set-ups that include lion-dance costumes and a bride being carried on a sedan chair in her wedding procession. Boys will especially enjoy seeing the cannons and other weaponry of old, as well as the scenes of historic battles that took place in Hong Kong.

Hong Kong Museum of History

Hong Kong Tourism Board

Any trip to Hong Kong should begin with a tour of the Museum of History, established in 1975, when the City Museum and Art Gallery split into two separate institutions: the Hong Kong Museum of Art and the Hong Kong Museum of History. Today the facility, which shares its complex with the Hong Kong Science Museum, has amassed more than 90,000 artifacts. The collection is divided into three major disciplines: natural history, ethnography and local history. The permanent exhibit, **Hong Kong Story**, gives a great overview of the area from Neolithic times to the transfer of sovereignty in 1997 – even if more recent times are not as thoroughly documented. Thanks to life-sized replicas, visitors can stroll through the **colonial streets of Hong Kong** with its old market stalls and restaurants. A Chinese medicine store that stood at 180 Queen's Road West has been reconstructed here piece by piece. Most of the furniture is from the 1885 period. In another part of the museum, you'll learn about the various Chinese cultures that coexist in the area; dioramas here invite you to step into the privacy of Hakka ceremonies or to peek inside a **sampan** used as a dwelling by the Tankas, or Boat People.

CULTURAL MUSEUMS

🍵 Museum of Teaware★★★
茶具文物館

Flagstaff House, Hong Kong Park, Admiralty. MTR: Admiralty. Open year-round Wed–Mon 10am–5pm. Closed holidays and the first three days of the Chinese New Year. 2869 0690/6690. www.lcsd.gov.hk.

Museum of Teaware

© Alex Havret/Apa Publications

Flagstaff House, thought to be the oldest colonial house remaining in Hong Kong – built in the 1840s – was both office and residence of the Commander of the British Forces in Hong Kong. It was converted to the Museum of Teaware in 1984, retaining its stately residential ambience while devoting its space to the display of tea ware.

Specializing in the collection, study and display of teaware, the museum's holdings date from the Tang Dynasty (618-907) to modern times. Here, tea lovers will find a wealth of information and collectors will be amazed by the elegance and originality of the teapots on display.

Among some of the most interesting are the exhibits on Chinese Tea Drinking that explain infusion techniques and methods of tea preparation through the ages. Astonishingly, these techniques go back to Neolithic times, and not all of them have roots in China. South Asia and Japanese tea cultures are also examined here, as are the Western preferences for tea.

Browse the small gift shop for teapots, tea, and books on the subject. And, if you have the time, come back for one of the many programs, including tea ceremonies and lectures, that the museum sponsors.

Hong Kong Heritage Museum★★
香港文化博物館

1 Man Lam Rd., Sha Tin, New Territories. MTR: Che Kung Temple (museum is a 5min walk from the station; follow signs). Open year-round Wed–Mon 10am–6pm (Sun & holidays until 7pm). Closed the first 2 days of the Chinese New

---

The Kung Fu of Tea

To the uninitiated, a Kung Fu Cha (or Gong Fu Cha) tea service looks like a toy tea set. Why use such tiny cups and such a small teapot? This method of preparation guarantees a flavorful brew. The teapot and cups are first boiled. Then the tea leaves are rinsed several times in boiling water before being served. Both an art and a convivial moment to be shared with family or friends, the act of drinking tea is meditative and the tea is enjoyed in small sips. Manufactured in Yixing in the Jiangsu province, the magnificent teapots used in Kung Fu Cha are highly prized by collectors.

Cantonese Opera Heritage Hall, Hong Kong Heritage Museum

Year. HK$10. 2180 8188.
www.heritagemuseum.gov.hk.
Along with the Hong Kong
Museum of History, this is one of
the not-to-be-missed museums in
the region. You'll discover several
sides to Hong Kong through the six
permanent exhibits.

Those in the **Cantonese Opera
Heritage Hall** give key pointers on
the interpretation of this art, along
with displays of bright costumes,
décor and musical instruments in a
reconstruction of an opera theater.
New Territories Heritage Hall
fascinates visitors interested in
history and urban development.
Covering some 6,000 years of the
region's history, the gallery also
includes a section on the various
ethnic groups that live in the area.
In the **T.T. Tsui Gallery of Chinese
Art**, you'll marvel at collections of
ceramics, bronze pieces and other
ancient objects.

Catering to kids ages 4 to 10, the
Children's Discovery Gallery
details Hong Kong's natural history
and archaeology. The museum
also organizes performances
of Cantonese opera, as well as
temporary exhibitions of local and
international art.

Hong Kong University Museum and Art Gallery★ 香港大學美術博物館

*94 Bonham Road, Pok Fu Lam,
Mid-Levels. From Central Star Ferry
bus stops, catch mini-bus no.8 or
22, or get a 3B double-decker bus
outside City Hall in Central. Open
daily 9:30am–6pm, Sun 1pm–6pm
Closed holidays and when the
university is not in session. 2241
5500. www.hku.hk/hkumag.*

Located in the West Mid-Level
heights, the University of Hong
Kong (founded in 1912) assembles
more than 8,000 students on its
verdant campus. In 1953, the
Fung Ping Shan Building was
converted into a museum; today
its remarkable **ceramic and
bronze** pieces – some dating from
the Neolithic period – delight
enthusiasts of Chinese history and
art. The museum also features the
largest collection of **Nestorian
crosses** from the Yuan Dynasty
(1271-1368) in the world.
Housed in the lower three stories
of the T.T. Tsui Building, the **art
gallery** holds changing exhibitions
of contemporary Hong Kong art.

75

Sun Yat-sen

Born in in Kwangtung (near Macau) in1866 to a Chinese farmer, Sun Yat-sen straddled the two worlds of the east and west. He eventually moved to Hawaii, where he attended college. By the time he moved back to Hong Kong to study medicine, he had become interested in politics and began to preach reform of the Manchu government.

Recognized as a revolutionary and a political leader in his own right, Sun Yat-sen played a role in the 1911 overthrow of the Qing Dynasty, the last imperial dynasty of China. He developed his Three Principles of the People – nationalism, democracy, and social reform – in an attempt to make China a free and prosperous nation. Unfortunately, Sun-Yat-sen did not live to see his party win power; he died of cancer in Beijing in 1925, and his party split into two factions after his death.

Dr. Sun Yat-sen Museum
孫中山紀念館

7 Castle Rd., Central. 2367 6373. hk.drsunyatsen.museum. MTR: Central. Open year-round Fri–Wed 10am–6pm (Sun & holidays until 7pm). HK$10.

This four-story museum is dedicated to the founding father of Republican China (*see sidebar, above*). The permanent exhibit here, **Dr. Sun Yat-sen and Modern China**, not only give a good general view of Sun Yat-sen's career, but also details the Hong Kong of his time through a collection of objects, archival documents and videos (with English subtitles).

The superb buildings of this 1919 **comprador house**, a mix of European and Chinese styles, were occupied beginning in 1971 by the Church of Jesus Christ of Latter-Day Saints; this explains the surprising presence of a baptistery on the ground floor.

The museum also presents a lecture and film series as well as crafts workshops (i.e., puppet and lantern making) for children.

Dr. Sun Yat-sen Museum

Florent Bonnefoy/Michelin

Hong Kong Heritage Discovery Centre

© Ian Trower / Alamy

Hong Kong Heritage Discovery Centre
香港文物探知館

In Kowloon Park, Haiphong Rd., Tsim Sha Tsui, Kowloon. MTR: Tsim Sha Tsui. Open year-round Fri–Wed 10am–6pm, Sun & holidays 10am–7pm. Closed Thu. 2208 4400. www.lcsd.gov.hk.

The Centre occupies the compact former Hong Kong History Museum site, originally built as Blocks S61 and S62 of the former Whitfield Barracks of the British Army (c.1910) at Kowloon Park. Now it is the public go-to resource for information about the conservation of Hong Kong's archaeological sites and existing historical structures. The Antiquities and Monuments Office strives to protect the territory's diverse cultural heritage. Since many of these heritage sites are in the New Territories, the Centre makes a good place to stop before planing your excursions outside Hong Kong Island. Spend some time browsing through the exhibition gallery, attend a talk in the lecture hall, or do research in the reference library. Admission to the Centre is free.

Lei Cheng Uk Han Tomb Museum
李鄭屋漢墓博物館

41 Tonkin St., Sham Shui Po, Kowloon. MTR: Cheung Sha Wan (then a 10min walk). Open daily 10am–6pm, Sun 1pm–6pm. Closed holidays. 2386 2863. www.lcsd.gov.hk.

Located within a gritty slice of Kowloon, the Han Dynasty (25-220) tomb featured here was discovered in 1955, when a hill being leveled turned out to be a burial chamber. The four vaulted chambers of the tomb – declared an official monument in 1988 – still contain bronze and pottery pieces. Though most of its interior is closed to the public for conservation reasons, visitors can still glimpse the tomb through the glass panel at the entrance passage.

In the **exhibition hall** adjacent to the tomb, you can see the pottery and bronze wares excavated from the tomb, as well as two displays. One describes the Lei Cheng Uk Han Tomb through text, videos and models, while the other focuses on the Han Dynasty architecture of South China.

CULTURAL MUSEUMS

PARKS AND GARDENS

Sometimes, in urban Hong Kong, it seems that lampposts pass for trees on the crowded streets. The government has tried to bring some greenery back – for instance on Nathan Road, where trees used to line the thoroughfare less than a century ago. Meanwhile, if your time and energy levels don't permit a climb of the nearest hill that pops up in the sea of concrete, you'll be glad to know that the city does have a few tranquil parks worth exploring.

In Kowloon, discounting the odd micro-parks with benches and plants that punctuate several neighborhoods, it's all about **Kowloon Park** – though **Kowloon Walled City Park** (*see Chinese Heritage Sites*) does also have some open space.

On Hong Kong Island, three significant green spaces provide a respite from their buzzing city surroundings: **Hong Kong Park★★**, **Hong Kong Zoological and Botanical Gardens★**, and **Victoria Park**. You can rise above it all for a walk around the circuit trail at **The Peak★★★** (*see Regions/Hong Kong Island North*), which has a few picnic tables and a children's playground. For a serious getaway, head to **Hong Kong Wetland Park** in the New Territories.

Hong Kong Park★★
香港公園

19 Cotton Tree Dr., Admiralty, Hong Kong Island. MTR: Admiralty. Open year-round daily 6am–11pm. 2521 5041. www.lcsd.gov.hk/parks/hkp.

This 8-hectare/20-acre park, set in the space next to Pacific Place Mall, offers a verdant escape in the heart of the city. Here, among fountains, ponds and waterfalls, you'll find a greenhouse overflowing with rare plants, a playground, and a viewing platform. Open since 1991, the park is also home to a popular wedding registry, making this a favored site in which to take wedding photographs. Older Hong Kongers practice tai chi alongside the children who play near the park's koi ponds.

Hong Kong Park encompasses one of the city's cultural gems, the **Museum of Teaware★★★** (*in Flagstaff House; see Cultural Museums*). Here, too, you'll find the

Edward Youde Aviary★ (*open year-round daily 9am–5pm; see Family Fun*). Named in memory of Sir Edward Youde, governor of Hong Kong from 1982 to 1986, the aviary incorporates elevated walkways that allow visitors to observe the birds at branch level.

Hong Kong Zoological and Botanical Gardens★
香港動植物公園

Albany Rd., Central. MTR: Central. Open year-round daily 6am–7pm (10pm for Fountain Terrace). 2530 0154. www.lcsd.gov.hk/parks.

Set on the northern slope of Victoria Peak, this zoo and botanical garden opened to the public back in 1864. Since then, the gardens have been expanded in phases into what is now a lush and mature oasis containing some 1,000 species of plants. Stroll the footpaths past fig trees, palms, azaleas, and a host of bright

MUST SEE

Bird Lake, Kowloon Park

Florent Bonnefoy/Michelin

flowers in the garden at **Fountain Terrace**. The site's small zoo and play-ground are popular with children (*see Family Fun*).

Hong Kong Wetland Park
香港濕地公園

Wetland Park Rd., Tin Shui Wai, New Territories. MTR: Tin Shui Wai; then take Light Rail 705 to Wetland Park Station. Open year-round Wed–Mon 10am–5pm. HK$30. 3152 2666. www.wetland park.com.

This 61-hectare/150-acre park was built partially to offset the encroachment of Tin Shui Wai New Town development into these unique wetlands. A world-class conservation and educational site, Hong Kong Wetland Park sits on the migratory path of several bird species and is home to some rare native Hong Kong fauna. Walk along the elevated paths and peek into bird hides where you might spot egrets, kingfishers and black-faced spoonbills.

In **Wetland Interactive World**, you'll find themed exhibition galleries, a theater and an indoor play area for young visitors.

Kowloon Park 九龍公園

Between Kowloon Park Dr. and Nathan Rd., Tsim Sha Tsui, Kowloon. MTR: Tsim Sha Tsui. Open year-round daily 5am– midnight. 2724 3344. www.lcsd.gov.hk/parks.

Hong Kong's largest recreational facility occupies the site of a former British military base (c.1860s). A haven of serenity for residents in the Tsim Sha Tsui and Jordan districts, the park contains three swimming pools, including one indoor, heated, Olympic-size pool. It's worth strolling through the Chinese-style gardens and visiting the **aviary** and the **bird lake**, where flamingos and other exotic species coexist. Also onsite are a fitness trail, two children's playgrounds and a maze garden. The southeast corner of the 13.5-hectare/33-acre Kowloon Park is known as the exercise grounds for practitioners of kung fu; and one of the park's old army barracks now houses the **Hong Kong Heritage Discovery Centre** (*see Cultural Museums*). Around noon every day, the park fills with the area's bankers and business people, who come to enjoy their lunch here.

Serene Spot for a Healthy Meal

Located at the western end of Nan Lian Garden, overlooking the Silver Strand waterfall from its tables, **Long Men Lou** (*3658 9388*) serves up wholesome vegetarian meals. Operated by the **Chi Lin Nunnery★★★** (which is supported by the eatery's profits), the restaurant is a charitable organization that started out providing nutritious meals to the needy in post-WWII Hong Kong more than 50 years ago. Chi Lin's kitchen has developed a unique contemporary vegetarian food culture and turns out tasty food for health-conscious diners. How do they do it? By combining quality natural ingredients with innovative preparation methods to create flavorful and attractively presented dishes. Expect rare mushrooms, a variety of tofu, and seasonal vegetables and fruits – all prepared to the highest standards, accented by fresh herbs and sauces. Lunch, dinner and afternoon tea menus are available.

Nan Lian Garden
南蓮園池

60, Fung Tak Rd., Diamond Hill, Kowloon. MTR: Diamond Hill. Open year-round daily 7am–5:30pm. 2329 8811. www.nanliangarden.org.

Located next to (and run by) the office of the **Chi Lin Nunnery★★★** (*see Chinese Heritage Sites*), the Nan Lian Garden is a designated public park, with an area of 35,000m²/380,000sq ft. The garden is built in the classical style of the Tang Dynasty (618 AD–907 AD), incorporating stylized hills, rocks, pools, plants and timber pavilions. In the distance, Lion Rock and its surrounding mountains to the north serve as a seamless backdrop. It's all a striking contrast to the polished Hollywood Plaza shopping mall, which connects to the MTR next to the park entrance. Free tours highlighting the park's natural, landscaped and structural features can be arranged. Temporary exhibitions of artwork, rare rocks and plants are sometimes held here too; there may be an admission fee for these.

Nan Lian Garden Bridge

Victoria Park
維多利亞公園

Victoria Park Rd., Causeway Bay, Hong Kong Island. MTR: Causeway Bay. Open year-round daily 24hrs. 2890 5824. www.lcsd.gov.hk/ parks/vp.

A welcome haven of greenery in a world of asphalt, Hong Kong's largest park (19 hectares/47 acres) was built in the 1950s and named for the statue of Queen Victoria that previously presided over Statue Square.

From morning until night, tai chi and kung fu practitioners come to train here, while older citizens often walk the paths, carrying their birds in cages.

On weekends, the park's two ponds become the place where the city's remote-control boat enthusiasts race their small gasoline-fueled vessels.

On Sundays, the whole place becomes the socializing ground for the city's Indonesian population, who gather here for picnics on their day off.

Annual events held at the park include a flower market during Chinese New Year, a lantern exhibition for the Mid-Autumn Festival, and an annual nighttime candlelight ceremony in memory of the Tiananmen Square massacre on June 4th.

Yuen Po Street Bird Garden 雀仔街

At the end of Flower Market Rd., Mong Kok, Kowloon. MTR: Prince Edward. Open year-round daily 7am–8pm.

A grand archway at the end of Flower Market Road announces the Yuen Po Street Bird Garden, formerly known as the **Bird Market** (*see Street Markets*). The market was renamed Yuen Po Street Bird Garden after it was sanitized and renovated with a little landscaped garden. This site is more interesting for people- and bird-watching (birds are prized pets in China), and a look at the ornate bird cages sold here than for the park itself.

Tai Chi

Many parks and waterfront spaces come alive with the slow, flowing, meditative movements of **tai chi** as day breaks across Hong Kong. It's not only the over-60 crowd who follow this practice. A martial art that developed in ancient China, tai chi's original name, tai chi chuan, means "the ultimate fist." This moving meditation is now practiced by people of all ages as a means to improve health. In Kowloon Park, free English-language introductory classes can be booked through the Hong Kong Tourism Board (*www.discoverhongkong.com*), and any hotel concierge can recommend good instructors.

Practicing Tai Chi

Florent Bonnefoy/Michelin

MACAU ★★★ 澳門

Located 60km/37mi southwest of Hong Kong in Guangdong province, Macau was the oldest European colony in China. The colony fell under Portuguese influence from 1567 to 1999. Today, Macau (a.k.a. Macao) displays its European heritage overtly in the historic center, now a UNESCO World Heritage Site. A decidedly Portuguese air holds sway here, in the quaint houses and Baroque churches, as well as in the cuisine – a fusion of Portuguese and Chinese. Elsewhere on the island, especially by night, the place pulsates to the sound of roulette wheels and slot machines.

A Colonial Past

In 1567 the Portuguese obtained Macau in exchange for rent paid to China, and soon established an outpost on the island. In the 16C, the port of Macau bustled with ships sailing between Europe, China and Japan. Also during this time, the territory became the Asian center for the Jesuits, who used Macau as a base from which to launch evangelical missions to Japan and China. It was the Jesuits who funded the building of the magnificent Baroque churches on the island.

All this wealth eventually spawned jealousy, especially on the part of the Dutch who destroyed the foundations of Portuguese trade in Asia by usurping the Indonesian spice trade. Macau declined further when the emperor of China opened the country's ports to international trade in 1684.

The Rise of Casinos

After the **First Opium War** (1839–1842), Macau's economy suffered when faced with competition from the deepwater ports of neighboring Hong Kong. In 1846 the new governor annexed the island of Taipa and authorized betting in order to increase the colony's income. The Chinese granted the sovereignty of Macau to the Portuguese in 1887.

Return to China

Portugal established diplomatic relations with the People's Republic of China when it was established in 1979, and Beijing subsequently acknowledged Macau as a "Chinese territory under Portuguese administration." The 29.5km²/11sq mi **Macau Special Administrative Region** (MSAR), with a current population of 556,800 people, was officially handed over to the PRC on December 20, 1999. With gambling tourism Macau's biggest source of revenue – making up about 50% of the economy – the MSAR today plays a significant role in the Hong Kong-Canton-Macau trio.

Ruins of St. Paul's Church

MACAU CENTER★★★

The island's historic core, on the Macau peninsula, preserves the charm of its Portuguese heyday in a collection of European-looking streets, squares, churches and government buildings erected during the 16th and 17th centuries. Declared a UNESCO World Heritage Site in 2005, the area where the Portuguese first settled in 1557 is one of the main attractions of a visit to this island (a trip of only an hour by ferry). Begin in **Largo do Senado★★★**, the heart of the early colony. As you walk through the area, you'll see Chinese temples interspersed with Baroque architecture in a lovely intermingling of East and West.

Largo do Senado★★★
議事亭前地

On Avenida de Almeida Ribeiro.

In this square, the heart of old Macau, you'll get your best taste of the island's four-plus centuries as a Portuguese colony. Also known as **Senate Square**, the pastel-colored pedestrian precinct is marked by a black and white mosaic wave-patterned square framed by the **Leal Senado★** ("loyal Senate") municipal compound, the General Post Office and the sunny yellow façade of **St. Dominic's Church★★★**.

The 1789 Leal Senado has housed the Institute of Civic and Municipal Affairs since 1999. Its architecture, which includes an interior courtyard whose walls are lined with *azulejo* ceramic tiles, is typically Portuguese.

Next to the bright white Santa Casa de Misericordia (Holy House of Mercy), a mission set up in 1568, is the yellow-hued **Pharmacia Popular**. Generations of Macanese have come here to stock up on Chinese and Occidental medicines. In the middle of the square, there is a small fountain, where Macanese residents habitually gather. You'll also find a small Macau tourism office here.

Ruins of St. Paul's Church★★★ 大三巴牌坊

Rua de São Paulo. 2835 3444. Crypt open daily year-round 7am–6pm.

Perching on a hill at the top of a flight of stairs like an eerie theater backdrop, this immense tiered stone façade is the only part of the church of São Paulo left standing. Even so, it is a masterpiece in itself. The icon, built by the Jesuits in the early 17C, was converted into an army barracks after the Jesuits were kicked out of Macau in 1762. The façade bears the scars of the 1835 fire that destroyed the rest of the structure, which, at the end of the 16C, was the largest church in Asia.

Touring Tip

The best way to discover Macau is on foot. If you ignore the obvious Chinese elements, you could easily imagine that you were in in a Portuguese city, surrounded by Old Word Baroque churches, especially around the **Largo do Senado★★★**. The south part of the peninsula is just as quaint. Take the time to stroll its little hillside streets and avenues, where some of Macau's most beautiful dwellings can be found.

EXCURSIONS

Take time to admire the wonderful **sculptures**★★★, carved over 25 years by Japanese Christian workers according to the designs of an Italian architect. At the top, a bronze dove, depicting the Holy Spirit, is surrounded by the sun and the moon. Beneath this, the infant Jesus is shown with symbols of the crucifixion. On the third tier, you'll see the Virgin Mary, along with angels and flowers, and a seven-headed Hydra being trampled by a woman (the Holy Mother). Among the flowers are peonies representing China, and chrysanthemums symbolizing Japan. Four statues of Jesuit saints stand in the lowest tier.

St. Dominic's Church★★★ 玫瑰聖母堂

Largo do Senado. Open year-round daily 10am–6pm.

One of the best examples of colonial Portuguese Baroque architecture, the stunning **Igreja de São Domingos** is recognizable by its green-shuttered yellow and white façade. Built in the 17C and renovated in 1997, the church incorporates elements of Asian design, such as the Chinese roof tiles. Inside, a statue of the Virgin Mary holding the Christ child occupies the place of honor above the cream-colored stone altar and appears to watch over worshippers here. The ceiling is adorned with the seal of St. Dominic, which also appears in other places around the sanctuary. The May 13th procession in honor of Our Lady of Fatima begins at this church (*see Calendar of Events*).

Kun Iam Temple★★ 觀音堂

Avenida do Coronel Mesquita. Open year-round daily 7am–6pm.

Dedicated to the Goddess of Mercy, called Kwan Yin in Cantonese, this temple dates from the 14C. Its **roof**★ is covered with painted statues representing historic scenes. The religious fervor of the worshippers of the goddess is apparent from the moment you set foot in the sanctuary. In the third prayer hall, the **statue of Kwan Yin**★ is decked out in pearls and the flowing robes of a young Chinese bride. She is surrounded by 18 *arhats*, or disciples of Buddha. The entire temple is decorated with paintings and statues of a rare quality. Most of

St. Dominic's Church

© Gouyan/Dreamstime.com

Lucky Marbles

While you're at Kun Iam Temple, don't hesitate to roll the marbles into the mouth of the lion at the main staircase. Roll them three times to the left for good luck.

MUST SEE MACAU

these represent Kwan Yin, dressed in white during various times of her life.

🛁 Lou Lim Ieoc Garden★★ 盧廉若公園

Estrada de Adolfo Loureiro. 2833 7676. Open daily 6am–9pm.

The house and the walled garden that surrounds it were built in the 19C by wealthy Chinese merchant Lou Kau. Modeled on the famed classical gardens of Suzhou, the garden features a nine-turn bridge that zigzags across the pond (according to legend, evil spirits can only move in straight lines) to a large pavilion combining classical and Chinese architectural elements. The pavilion also hosts concerts during the annual Macau International Music Festival (*see Calendar Of Events*). Now an art gallery, the house has a covered terrace facing the pond. Benches here make tranquil places to take a break from sightseeing.

Museum of Macau★ 澳門博物館

112 Praceta do Museu de Macao. Entrance via escalator next to St. Paul's ruins. 2835 7911. www.macaumuseum.gov.mo. Open year-round Tue–Sun 10am–6pm. MOP15.

Built into the side of the 17C **Monte Fortress★** 大炮臺 (*Fortaleza do Monte*), east of the St. Paul's ruins, the Museum of Macau retraces the historical progression of China and Europe up to the 16C. Three floors of permanent exhibits limn the beginnings of Macau and examine early Macanese life, including politics,

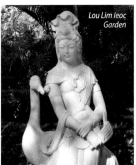

Lou Lim Ieoc Garden

Glyn Genin/Apa Publications

cultural development, folk customs and festivals, as well as arts and crafts. Particularly interesting is how the museum compares the Chinese and European cultures in the 16C, the time when they first encountered each other. Displays on the third floor bring history up to the present with a look at modern-day Macau.

🛁 Guia Fortress & Chapel 東望洋炮台

Estrada de Cacilhas (access through Avenida de Sidonio Pais). Open year-round daily 9am–5:30pm.

Take the cable car to the top of Guia Hill (*MOP$3*), site of a 17C fortress and an 1865 lighthouse – the first on the China coast. Completed in 1638, the fortress was originally supposed to defend the border with China, but was mainly used as a surveillance post. The 17C **chapel★** is adorned wtih pink and blue frescoes of Portuguese and Chinese inspiration, as well as a statue of the Virgin Mary. Legend has it that the Virgin left her shrine and deflected Dutch bullets with her dress during an attack in 1662.

EXCURSIONS

85

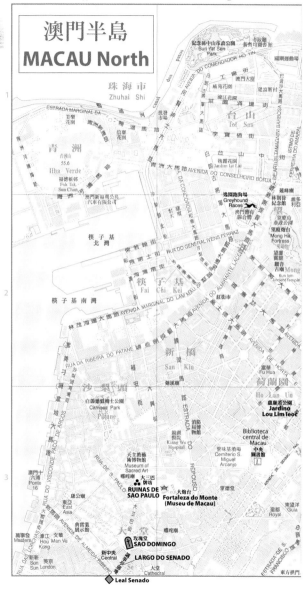

澳門半島
MACAU North

珠海市
Zhuhai Shi

ESTRADA MARGINAL DA

美景
花園
信盛

青 洲
青洲山
55.6
Ilha Verde
福德斯郊
Fok Tak
Sun Chun
澳門福利公共
汽車有限公司

氹子基
北灣

氹 子 基
Fai Chi Kei

氹子基南灣

RUA DA RIBEIRA DO PATANE

沙 梨 頭
Patane

白頭墳賈梅士公園
Camoes Park

天主教藝
術博物館
Museum of
Sacred Art

噴吔廟 大 三 巴 牌坊
**RUINAS DE
SAO PAULO**

澳門
六街口
Ponte
16

東亞
East
Asia

葡華發
Masters Co
港江 文華
Hou Man Va
Kong

與牌業
東方葡萄牙

大堂
玫瑰堂
SAO DOMINGO
新中央
Central
LARGO DO SENADO
大堂
Se
Cathedral

◆ **Leal Senado**

CANAL dos Patos

AVENIDA DO COMENDADOR HO YIN
紀念孫中山市政公園
Sun Yat Sen
Park
市政總
署臨時
城市活動館
閱瀾運動館

澳門工業街
工業街
嫩苑花園
渡江花園
建富新村

台 山
Toi San

實惠街

青洲大馬路 AVENIDA DO CONSELHEIRO BORJA
白台山 中
逸麗花園
Jardim Iat Lai

逸園跑狗場
**Greyhound
Races**
澳門跑狗
場有限公司

林則徐
紀念館

翠鴻地
市政公園
望廈炮台
**Mong Ha
Fortress**

望廈
觀音
古廟 Mong
Kun Iam
Ancient Temple

RUA DO GENERAL IVENS FERRAZ

AVENIDA DO ALMIRANTE LACERDA

新 橋
San
Kiu

紅街市

AVENIDA DE HORTA E

富華
Fu Hua

荷蘭園
Ho Lan Un

盧廉若公園
**Jardino
Lou Lim Ieoc**

消防局
博物館

鏡湖
醫院
Kiang Wu
Hospital

聖珠基墳場
Cemiterio S.
Miguel
Arcanjo

Biblioteca
central de
Macau
中央
圖書館

ESTRADA DO REPOUSO

望德堂

大炮台
**Fortaleza do Monte
(Museu de Macau)**

噴吔廟

園裡
Royal

東望洋
Royal

ESTRADA DE S. FRANCISCO

東方拱門

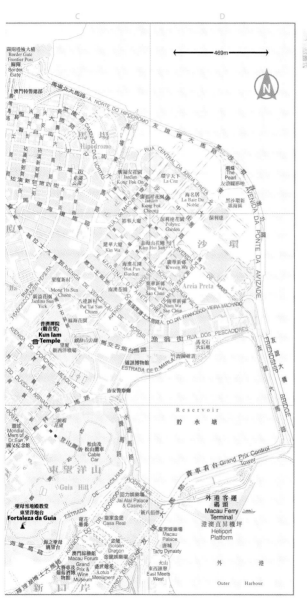

EXCURSIONS

Facing the port, the area south of Largo do Senado was for many years the heart of Macau. Today a quiet ambience pervades this hillside district.

A-Ma Temple★★★
荷李活道

Rue de S. Tiago da Batra. Open year-round daily 7am–6pm.

A-Ma and Hong Kong's Tin Hau are the same: the young girl from Fujian who saved her brothers from drowning – now the goddess who protects sailors. The 17C building is festooned with red walls and green roofs adorned by pieces of varnished porcelain. Inside, the boat sculpted in stone represents the one that the goddess used to save the sailors.

Avenida da Praia Grande★★ 南灣大馬路
Surrounded by banyan trees, this walkway – where locals once came to admire the sea – now sits back from the water. Note the colonial house with the rose-colored façade; this is the 19C residence of the former governor.

Avenida da Republica★★ 民國大馬路
Winding around the southern shore of Nam Van Lake, this tree-shaded avenue is lined with pretty Macanese houses.

St. Augustine Square ★
崗頂前地
This triangular courtyard, a.k.a **Largo de Santo Agostinho**, is home to the Cultural Institute of Macau. Also bordering the square is the baroque-style 1814 **St. Augustine Church**, famed for its white marble statue of Christ carrying the cross. Nearby, on Rue de São Lourenco, stands **St. Lawrence Church**. Peek inside for a look at the lovely painted ceiling.

Rua da Felicidade★
福隆新街
Running parallel to the Avenida de Almeida Ribeiro, this once-sleazy street is now known for its pastries and affordable guest houses. The street's white storefronts stood in for Shanghai in the movie *Indiana Jones and the Temple of Doom*, which was filmed here in 1984.

Macau Maritime Museum 海事博物館

11 Largo do Pagode da Barra. 2540 0350. www.museumaritimo.gov. mo. Open year-round Wed–Mon 10am–6pm. MOP10 (Sun MOP5).

Opposite the A-Ma Temple, this museum will appeal to those who love ships and the sea. Displays include a collection of scale-model ships as well as a life-sized model of a Chinese dragon boat.

🚠 Macau Tower
澳門旅遊塔

Largo da Torre de Macau. 2893 3339. Open year-round daily 10am–9pm. MOP120 www. macautower.com.

Close to the edge of Nam Van Lake, Macau Tower rises 338m/1,109ft above the island. Take the high-speed glass-front elevator up to the observation platform. From here, if the weather is clear, you can see across Macau all the way to the Chinese border.

MUST SEE MACAU

THE ISLANDS

While Taipa and Colôane islands used to lie off the peninsula of Macau, they are now linked to the mainland by three bridges and connected to each other by a strip of reclaimed land called the Cotai Strip – site of many of the newer casino hotels. It's only a matter of time before all three places are completely integrated into the peninsula. Peaceful Colôane has so far escaped development, and is still known for its little village and pleasant beaches.

Taipa 氹仔島

There are two ways to visit Taipa. One is to casino hop on the **Cotai Strip** and hedge your bets in one of the largest gambling areas in the world. Or forsake the modern for a stroll back in time in the original **village of Taipa** at the southern tip of the island. Streets here resemble a typical Portuguese village and hold some of the best Macanese-Portuguese fusion restaurants.

Taipa Houses Museum

© TI_to_tito/Dreamstime.com

Taipa Houses Museum ★
龍環葡韻住宅博物館
Avenida da Praia. Open Tue–Sun 10am–6pm. MOP5. 2882 7103. www.iacm.gov.mo/museum.
The five early-20C colonial villas that make up the **Casas Museu de Taipa** used to overlook magnificent stands of mangrove trees, which were lost when Cotai was developed. Built for high-ranking civil servants and Macanese families, the houses are now museums, furnished as they would have been in the 1920s.

🚢 Colôane 路環島

A tranquil atmosphere prevails in the village of Colôane, which is much less developed than Taipa and connected to it via a large parcel of reclaimed land known as the **Cotai Strip**.
Once a hideaway for pirates, the village is now apeaceful haven. Take time to stroll through the picturesque streets, especially in late afternoon, or hike on

Lord Stowe's Bakery

1 Rua de Tassara, Colôane Town Square. 2888 2534. www.lordstow.com.

A trip to Colôane is not complete without sampling one of Andrew Stowe's justifiably famous **egg tarts**, which are a tasty takeoff on the *pastéis de nata* made in Lisbon, Portugal. If you're on the Cotai Strip, look for Lord Stowe's new location in the Grand Canal Shoppes at The Venetian resort.

one of the eight marked trails. The beaches of this island, the southernmost of the SAR of Macau, attract hordes of tourists.

Chapel of St. Francis Xavier★
聖方濟各聖堂

Rua do Meio.

In the main square of Colôane Village, with its Portuguese mosaic paving and rows of neoclassical arcades, you'll find the **Chapel of São Francis Xavier**.

Though the chapel was built in 1928 to enshrine the arm bone of the saint and the remains of Christian martyrs from Japan, Korea and Indochina, these relics have since been moved.

Beaches

Buses 15 (A-Ma Temple), 21A or 26A (Largo do Senado and Avenida de Almeida Ribeiro), from Peninsula Macau.

Colôane Island is home to several beaches, which are easily accessible by bus or taxi. The first along the way, **Cheoc Van Beach**, sits in front of the Poussada de Colôane (*see HOTELS*). The bus route terminates at **Hác Sá**, a beach blanketed in black sand (colored by the silt of the Pearl River estuary). The color is being diluted little by little by the yellow sand that the government brings in to fight erosion. You can rent pedal boats at the **Water Activities Centre** (*8988 4118*) at Hác-Sá Reservoir, behind the Hác-Sá Picnic Park on the main road above the beach.

Tam Kung Temple 譚公聖廟
Avenida de Cinco de Outubro.

Along the Colôane shore, this temple is dedicated to Tam Kung – a Taoist god who protects sailors. Inside are two unusual treasures from the sea: a representation of a dragon boat, complete with men rowing, sculpted from a 1m/3ft-long whale bone; and the jaw of a giant shark caught offshore by local fishermen.

House of Dancing Water

City of Dreams, Cotai. MOP380. thehouseofdancingwater.com. Billing itself as the world's largest water-based show, this extravaganza at City of Dreams was conceived by Franco Dragone (the Italian-born showman who founded the Cirque de Soleil in Montreal). House of Dancing Water is performed by a cast of 77 acrobats, dancers, stuntmen and musicians in a custom-built 2,000-seat theater-in-the-round, which features a 14.1-liter/3.7-million-gallon pool, 258 automated fountains, and special elevators that convert the aquatic stage into a solid floor.

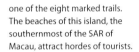

SHOPPING

Shopping in this duty-free port pales in comparison to Hong Kong, but there are still some good buys to be found – and with the slew of new casino hotels come more designer labels.

Antiques & Crafts

Antique shops cluster among the streets between the Largo do Senado and the ruins of São Paulo – as well as in Colôane Village.

Fisherman's Wharf

Avenida da Amizade. 8299 3300. www.fishermanswharf.com.mo. Open daily 10am–8pm.
Five minutes from the Hong Kong ferry terminal, this wharfside complex boasts an array of local and international shops.

Horta e Costa

This long road, stretching from the Red Market to Flora Park, is a local favorite for shopping. Just off Horta e Costa, **Fortune Tower Shopping Centre** *(70, Avenida do Ouvidor Arriaga)* is the largest computer market in Macau.

Red Market

Corner of Avenida Almirante Lacerda and Avenida Horta e Costa. Open daily 10am–7pm.
Built in 1936 in Art Deco style, this architectural heritage site has housed a dynamic mix of traders ever since. Stalls sell typical Pearl River Delta foodstuffs; jars of pickled vegetables make good gifts for foodies back home.

Rotunda Carlos da Maia

South of Avenida de Horta e Costa.
The area around this circular road on the peninsula is a favorite local browsing spot for clothing, fabric and jewelry. **Veng Fai** and **Mei Hou Commercial Centers** overflow with outlets selling cheap apparel, cosmetics and accessories.

Taipa Flea Market

Taipa Island.
Every Sunday *(9am–6pm)* this market touting handicrafts, toys, clothes and other souvenirs, holds sway in the village center between Bombeiros and Camões squares.

Resort Shopping

Macau's swanky hotels and resorts have equally glitzy shopping arcades, with the same designer names you'll see in Hong Kong malls. Serious shoppers should head for the wealth of retail stores at the exclusive **Shoppes at Four Seasons** *(Cotai Strip; www.shoppesatfourseasons.com)*; **The Venetian Macao**'s **Grand Canal Shoppes** *(Cotai Strip; www.grandcanalshoppes.com.mo)* and the **Wynn Esplanade** *(Rua Cidade de Sintra, Nape district; www.wynnmacau.com)*.

Fruit of the Vine

Portuguese wine is sold in grocery stores in Macau, but for the finest selection, head for the formidable cellars at the **Macau Wine Museum** *(Tourism Activities Centre, 431 Rua Luis Gonzaga Gomes; 8798 4188; open Wed–Mon 10am–6pm; MOP15 includes admission and tastings)*, where you can experience Portuguese wines first-hand.

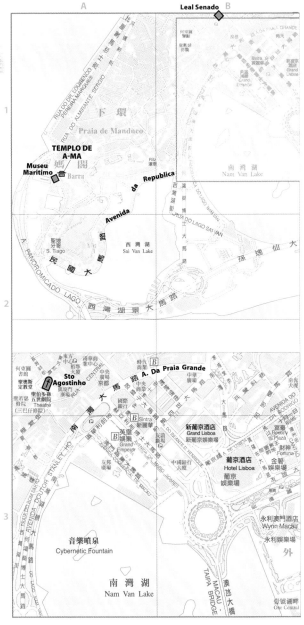

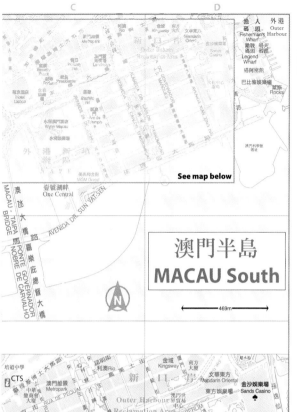

NIGHTLIFE

Aside from the Cotai Strip, bars and clubs cluster around **Avenida Sun Yat-sen**, Macau's party district. If you're a player, you'll feel right at home at one of Macau's 30-plus casinos, which stay open 24 hours.

Bars and Nightclubs

Club Cubic

2015-02, The Boulevard, City of Dreams, Estrada do Itsmo, Cotai. 6638 4999. www.cubic-cod.com.
Newly renovated and very swish, Cubic is Macau's super-club. Two main dance areas play house, electronic, funk, hip-hop and more. Dress to impress.

Playboy Club Macao

Sands Macao Hotel, 203 Largo de Monte Carlo. 8983 3388. www.playboymacao.com.
Decked out like an opulent penthouse apartment, this US franchise – complete with Playboy's signature "bunnies," is proving popular with women as well as men, who both enjoy it as an over-the-top night out.

Casinos

City of Dreams Casino

Estrada do Istmo, Cotai. 8868 6688. www.cityofdreamsmacau.com.
There's plenty to keep the visitor busy at this relative newcomer: 378 gaming tables, 1,122 slot machines, and a relaxed atmosphere to boot.

The Galaxy

Cotai Strip. 2888 0888. www.galaxymacau.com.
As the name suggests, all is glittering at this new casino-resort complex, which opened in May 2011. The resort boasts an artificial beach and 50 restaurants, while

the casino entertains 24/7 with more than 450 gaming tables.

Hotel Lisboa

2-4 Avenida de Lisboa. 2888 3888. www.hotellisboa.com.
One of Macau's original casinos, Lisboa was given a facelift when the US operations joined the fray. The main three-story building was topped in 2007 by an additional 58 floors to become the Grand Lisboa.

Hotel Lisboa

© Florent Bonnefoy/Michelin

Sands

203 Largo de Monte Carlo, Peninsula Macau. 2888 3388. www.sands.com.mo.
Sands was the first foreign casino to open in Macau in 2004. It has enjoyed success ever since, in the form of visitors from PRC who flock to the casino, only to leave their hard-earned money behind.

The Venetian Macao

Estrada da Baía de Nossa Senhora da Esperança, Taipa. 2882 8888. www.venetianmacao.com.
Claiming bragging rights to being the largest casino in the world, The Venetian boasts 51,000m²/548,960sq ft of gaming space, filled with some 3,400 slot machines and 800 game tables.

MUST SEE MACAU

SPAS

With the influx of new casino hotels on the Cotai Strip, Macau has no lack of places to be pampered. Resort spas below are open to the public.

Isala Spa

*Grand Hyatt Macau,
City of Dreams, Estrada do Istmo,
Cotai. 8868 1193. macau.grand.
hyatt.com.*
Whether you want to relax, re-energize, hydrate or detoxify, Isala Spa has just the right treatment. From a jade stone massage to a sweet lychee body scrub, you'll be transported at Isala.

Spa at the Four Seasons Macau

Four Seasons Hotel Macao, Cotai Strip®

Malo Clinic Health & Wellness

The Venetian Macau, Estrada da Baía de N. Senhora da Esperança, Taipa. 8862 2688. www.maloclinics.com.mo.
Opened in 2010, this 7,896m²/85,000sq ft integrative wellness complex combines a medical clinic, a beauty spa and a fitness facility. Think of it as one-stop shopping for all your wellness needs.

Six Senses Spa at MGM Macau

MGM Macau, 3/F Avenida Dr. Sun Yat-sen, Nape, Macau. 8802 3838. www.sixsenses.com.
Traditional Chinese medicine therapies, such as Tui Na and Shiatsu, complement Balinese and Thai-inspired treatments in this contemporary setting. Indulge in one of the elemental rituals; then kick back in the flotation pool.

Spa at the Four Seasons Macau

Estrada da Baía de N. Senhora da Esperança, Cotai Strip, Taipa. 2881-8888. www.fourseasons.com/macau/spa.
For a real indulgence, the Four Seasons Spa offers the Diamond

Magnetic Jewel ritual. Gem stones are first applied to the chakra points to clear your *qi* (energy) pathways. After your body is polished with crushed diamonds and micronized iron, magnets create a positive aura around you.

The Spa at Mandarin Oriental Macau

Avenida Dr. Sun Yat Sen, Nape, Macau. 8805 8888. www.mandarinoriental.com.
Boasting water views from its relaxation lounge, this sanctuary puts its guests back in balance using a combination of ancient and modern techniques.

The Spa at Wynn

Rua Cidade de Sintra, Nape, Macau. 2888 9966. www.wynnmacau.com.
Asian-inspired décor fashions a tranquil ambience at the spa in Wynn Tower. Here, the specially blended oils and deep pressure of a Macanese massage will release any tension you may be feeling, while just the name of the Deluxe Caviar Therapy will make you feel richer.

EXCURSIONS

Macau - Practical Information

When to Go

Macau shares a subtropical climate with Hong Kong. The temperature varies little, but there is a high level of humidity (see Practical Information to the front of this guide)**.**

Entrance Formalities

If you are coming from continental China and wish to return there after your trip to Macau, make sure you have obtained a **multi-entry visa**; if not, you will have to request a new visa (available through most travel agencies, such as the **China Travel Service** (see p97); or through the **Commissioner's Office of China's Foreign Ministry in the Macao SAR** (992 Av. do Dr. Rodrigo Rodrigues; open Mon–Fri 9am–noon & 2:30pm–5pm; no applications accepted Fri afternoon; 8791 5106 or 8791 5123/24hr line; www.fmcoprc.gov.mo). Visas are usually issued in 2, 3 or 4 days. **Consulates** have both Hong Kong and Macau under their jurisdiction.

Macau Government Tourist Office (MGTO) – 335-341 Alameda Dr. Carlos d'Assumpcao, Edificio "Hot Line," 12th floor. 2831 5566. www.macautourism.gov.mo/en.

Open Mon–Fri 9am–1pm, 2:30pm–5:45pm. Several information centers are scattered throughout the city, including at the Macau Ferry Terminal (open Mon–Fri 9am–10pm).

Getting There

By Plane

Macau International Airport – On the island of Taipa; 2181 8888; www.macau-airport.gov.mo. You will have to go through customs when you enter Macau.

Airlines

◆ **Air Macau** – 398 Alameda Dr. Carlos D'Assumpcao, Edif. CNAC, 13th floor; 8396 5555, www.airmacau.com.mo. Open Mon–Sat, except holidays 9am–6pm.

◆ **Air Asia** – Macau International Airport, Passenger Terminal, Mezzanine Level, Taipa; 080 0912; www.airasia.com.

Airport Taxis

From the airport, you'll pay about MOP50 for a taxi to Macau center. Several bus lines can also transport you to the center (MOP3.30). If you are staying in a large hotel, check to see if there is a free air-port shuttle.

The Right Gesture

Both the Hong Kongese and Macanese are familiar with Occidental customs, and won't be offended if you commit a few errors. To start off on the right foot, here are a few rules to observe:

◆ Shake the hands of men and women alike.
◆ Thank the waiter or waitress by tapping discreetly on the table with your index finger.
◆ Give trinkets as gifts to your friends when you return from a voyage.
◆ If you are invited to dinner, bring fruit and not flowers.

MACAU

MUST SEE

By Bus

♦ Kee Kwan Motor Road Co.
(*2893 3888; www.keekwan.com*)
runs bus service between Macau and
Guangdong 7:15am– 9:30pm. Buses
depart for Canton every 15min from
next to the Master Hotel (*corner of
Avenida Almeida Ribeiro & Rua das
Lorchas; 2hrs; MOP70*).

♦ China Travel Service (CTS)
(223-225 Avenida do Dr. Rodrigo
Rodrigues, Edif. Nam Kuong;
*2870 0888; www.cts.com.mo [travel
agency] and ctsbus.hkcts.com [bus
service]*) departs for Canton every
15min, 8:30am–9:20pm from
Metropark and Beverly Plaza hotels;
or every hour from the Grandview
Hotel (*2hrs; MOP75*).

For trips on the Macau peninsula,
a **ticket** costs MOP3.20. To reach
Taipa, it will cost MOP4.20; for
Coloane, MOP5; for Hác Sá Beach,
MOP6.40. To reach Colôane and
Taipa, take the bus directly from the
Ferry jetty or near Hotel Lisboa.

By Ferry

**Most of the ferries serving Macau
come from Hong Kong.**
♦ Macao Ferry Terminal–
Avenida da Amizade. Departure
for Hong Kong with TurboJet (*1hr;
HK150*) and New World First Ferry
(*1hr15min; HK150*).
**♦ Macao Taipa Temporary Ferry
Terminal** – (*5min by shuttle from
The Venetian hotel*). Departs
for Hong Kong every 30min,
7am–11:30pm; then at 1am,
3am and 5am.

Maritime Companies

♦ TurboJet – *8790 7039;
www.turbojet.com.hk.*

♦ New World First Ferry –
2872 7676; www.nwff.com.hk.
♦ Cotai Jet – *2885 0595;
cotaijet.com.mo.*

Basic Information

Emergencies

Emergency calls: 999
**♦ Conde de São Januário
Hospital (CHCSJ)** – Estrada do
Visconde de San Januáriom, Macau
Peninsula; *8390 5000 or 2831 3731;
www.ssm.gov.mo.* Some doctors
here speak basic English.

Internet

If you can't easily find a an
Internet café in Macau, computers
are available at the **Biblioteca
Central de Macao** (89A-B Avenida
Conselheiro Ferreira de Almeida;
*2856 7576 or 2855 8049; www.library.
gov.mo*) and the **Unesco Centre
of Macao** (Alameda d'Assumpção,
in the Nape district of Macau;
2872 7058).

Languages

Chinese and **Portuguese** are
the official languages of Macau.
Cantonese is also widely spoken.

Money

The **currency** in Macau is the
pataca (MOP). It is divided into
100 *avos*. The exchange rate is set
according to the Hong Kong dollar.
HK\$1 = PTC1.03. In July 2011, US\$1
= MOP8. Hong Kong dollars are
accepted in Macau.

Telephone

Macau prefix: 00 853 from other
countries and continental China;
or **00 86** for continental China.

OUTLYING ISLANDS 離島

Just 30 minutes from Central by boat, a whole other world awaits. Technically part of the New Territories, the Outlying Islands comprise 23 populated islands out of the more than 230 islets scattered in the waters around Hong Kong. Of those that are inhabited, Lantau★, Cheung Chau★★★ and Lamma★ are the most accessible and are popular for their lovely beaches, seafood restaurants and hiking trails. Give yourself at least a day to see these islands; you could easily spend a full day on Lantau alone.

🪷 CHEUNG CHAU ISLAND ★★★
長洲島

Outlying Ferry Pier Number 5, Central Piers. MTR: Tung Chau.

With its fishing village, port, and its historic Bun Festival (*see sidebar, below*), Cheung Chau still thrives on its old traditions. When you step off the ferry in the village, market stalls offer snacks that will tickle your taste buds – stuffed steamed buns, dumplings, noodles and fish balls. If you arrive early enough (before 9am), the port, filled with fishing boats of every color, looks like a postcard. Cheung Chau is especially renowned for its salted dry fish, *ham yu*, which is used liberally in Cantonese cookery; you will see it drying all over the place.

Some shops sell paper replicas of Vuitton bags, cell phones and houses; these are not toys, but offerings for the ancestors. The Chinese burn their dead to assure them a comfortable afterlife. Tradition dictates that one send paper money and food with the deceased, but inhabitants of Hong Kong, always up to date on the newest trends, prefer to burn renditions of the latest MP3 player. Even if you're dead, you don't have to be unfashionable!

LAMMA ISLAND ★
南丫島

Outlying Ferry Pier Number 5, Central Piers. MTR: Tung Chau.

Like Cheung Chau and Peng Chau, the third-largest island in Hong

---

Bun Festival

Each May, the **Bun Festival** takes place around the temple of Pak Tai. Its origins go back to the beginning of the 20C, when, after a series of unfortunate events, the islanders decided to make offerings of buns stuffed with lotus paste to the spirits of the dead. After these offerings were made, their luck came back, so they made a ritual of it.

Every year, three 13m/42.5ft-high bamboo towers are raised in front of the temple and covered with sweet buns. Taoist priests then order the wandering spirits to return to their own world, which they supposedly do after consuming the essence of the buns. During the festival, the villagers organize a procession that incorporates lion dancing and "floating" children. The latter represent mythical characters, which, cleverly attached to concealed wire frames, appear to float through the air.

There's nothing easier than getting to the Outlying Islands. Ferries to Cheung Chau, Lamma, Lantau and Peng Chau leave from Outlying Ferry Piers 1–6 in Central, next the Star Ferry Piers on Hong Kong Island (*30min–1hr each way*). Lamma ferries going back to Central stop operating from Yung Shue Wan at 11:30pm, and earlier from Sok Kwa Wan. Call or check online for schedules and information:

Ferries to Cheung Chau, Peng Chau and Mui Wo on Lantau – *2131 8181; www.nwff.com.hk.*

Ferries to Lamma – *2815 6063; www.hkkf.com.hk.*

Lamma Island

Florent Bonnefoy/Michelin

Kong is laced by foot paths. No cars are allowed on Lamma (except emergency vehicles), and bicycles are the favored mode of transport in this laid-back place.

The main village, **Yung Shue Wan**, features a handful of restaurants along its waterfront, as well as a few small hotels. From here, take the asphalt road in the direction of the other port village port on the island, **Sok Kwu Wan**, where seafood restaurants dish up the likes of chili crab, garlic prawns and steamed fish.

Beaches

From Yung Shue Wan, a trail passes **Tai Wan To**, known locally as "Power Station Beach" for the coal-fired generators that stand there. Next comes **Hung Shing Ye** beach, which offers showers and changing rooms. The path continues to the south and ends at the jetty of Sok Kwu Wan. Try to arrive in time to enjoy a seafood meal before boarding the ferry back to Central.

A hidden treasure, the quiet beach of **Lo Lo Shing★** has a lifeguard on duty (*follow the signs near Sok Wa Wan*). Nearby you'll find caves that were used by the Japanese kamikaze fighters in WWII. The caves contained motorboats filled with explosives ready to launch themselves on Allied ships (on-site signage tells the story).

LANTAU ISLAND★ 爛頭

Outlying Ferry Pier Number 6, Central Piers. MTR: Tung Chau.

The largest island in the area, Lantau is twice the size of its neighbor, Hong Kong Island. In recent years, Lantau has been developed and linked to Kowloon by road. Chek Lap Kok, an islet off the coast of Lantau, holds the international airport, while Penny's Bay is home to **Hong Kong Disneyland★★** (*see Theme Parks*). At Lantau's center, **Po Lin Monastery★** can now also be reached by cable car.

Po Lin Monastery★
寶蓮禪寺

Ngong Ping. From Mui Wo, bus 2; from Tung Chau MTR, bus 23; or take the Ngong Ping 360 cable car (see sidebar, below).

The first thing you'll want to do is climb the steps leading up to the seated bronze **Big Buddha**, which has loomed over the monastery since 1993. At 34m/111ft high, the statue is one of the largest representations of Buddha in China. Buddha is represented sitting on a throne in the shape of a lotus, surrounded by six smaller statues depicting the immortals that bring him offerings. Noble and serene, the statue raises one of his hands in a sign of appeasement of suffering, while the other hand rests on his hip as a gesture of offering.

Inside the Buddha, four paintings depict his spiritual journey (if you purchase the ticket that includes a meal at the dining hall, you can access a second exhibition area). Monks and nuns here led a tranquil existence in a modest setting until the 1970s, when the monastery was opened to the public. Since that time, the buildings have been expanded and the flow of visitors has never ceased.

Big Buddha, Po Lin Monastery

© A. Booth/ Fotolia.com

Tai O★ 大澳

From Mui Wo, bus no.1; from Tung Chau MTR station, take bus no. 11.

One of the last remaining fishing villages on Lantau island, Tai O was built on pilings by the Tankas, members of a South China fishing community that once lived aboard boats in the harbor here; some of their dwellings have been preserved. Tai O partially developed on the islet of the same name, which is now linked to Lantau by a bridge. There you will find the 16C **Temple of Kwan Tai**, god of loyalty and justice. Before you leave, make time for a meal at one of Tai O's seafood restaurants.

View from the Heavens

A dramatic cable car route stretches from Tung Chung, nearly 6km/3.7mi up the mountainside to the Ngong Ping Plateau, just a few minutes by foot from Po Lin and its big Buddha. The 25-minute ride on the **Ngong Ping 360 Sightseeing Cable Car** (*MTR: Tung Chung; 3666 0606; www.np360.com.hk*) affords views beyond Lantau and the airport all the way to urban Hong Kong. Around the Ngong Ping terminus there are cafés and nature trails, as well as high-tech educational displays related to Buddhist teachings. For a real treat, book the Crystal Cabin; its transparent floor makes views over the forested hillsides and the South China Sea all the more amazing.

MUST SEE OUTLYING ISLANDS

Take a Junk

If you're traveling with a group, consider hiring a junk (a small wooden pleasure boat), as a laid-back way to island-hop (*prices start at HK$3,000 for a half-day charter*). Hotel concierges can recommend reliable tour operators. A junk cruise is the only way to reach the most remote islets, such as Po Toi in the southern reaches of Hong Kong's territorial waters – a 3.7sq km/1.4 sq mi backwater with two restaurants in the hamlet that surrounds its pier. Some boat companies offer catering packages, so you can spend a half or a whole day on the water, complete with meals – a most pleasurable experience. Snorkeling equipment may also be available to explore the outer reaches of Hong Kong's waters, which swim with colorful marine life.

Mui Wo 梅窩

Though Lantau Island is now accessible by MTR from the new town of Tung Chung, the ferry that shuttles back and forth from Hong Kong Island is a more leisurely way to approach Lantau. The ferry stops at Mui Wo, a harbor village on the east coast of the island, known for pretty **Silvermine Bay Beach★**. The silver mine that made the village prosperous is long closed, but the pleasant stroll that takes you to the now-closed site passes near a rushing waterfall. In Mui Wo village, you can rent **bikes** and set off on your own adventure.

PENG CHAU ISLAND 坪洲

Outlying Ferry Pier Number 6, Central Piers.

Accessible by ferry from Central, or a short hop from Lantau by *keido*, a small wooden ferry, is the sparsely populated, one-square-kilometer (half a square mile) island of Peng Chau. This place oozes old Southern Chinese charm and can easily be explored on foot. Head for the central hill for a good view. The bars and restaurants near the pier are as relaxed as the islands off Hong Kong get.

Dragon Boat, Silvermine Bay

Florent Bonnefoy/Michelin

EXCURSIONS

THE GREAT OUTDOORS

Although the population is constantly growing, Hong Kong's generally hilly and mountainous topography means that some 70 percent of the territory is unspoiled countryside. Designated Country Parks abound in every corner of Hong Kong, but most of them can be found in the New Territories. **Hong Kong Geopark** is one of the most dramatic, closely rivaled by the natural beauty surrounding **Tai Long Wan beach** (see Beaches). Hikers can scale The **Dragon's Back★** hiking trail on Hong Kong Island, or attempt all or part of the 50km/31mi **Hong Kong Trail** that traverses the island's five country parks from Victoria Peak to Big Wave Bay. And for the great urban outdoors, the view of the cityscape from **Tsim Sha Tsui Promenade★★** (see Regions/Kowloon) is hard to beat.

Dragon's Back★

South part of Hong Kong Island. MTR: Shau Kei Wan; then take bus no. 9 in the direction of Shek O. Get off at the stop just after the little roundabout and go up the staircase.

Dragon's Back takes its name from the bumpy spine traced by this 8km/5mi trail on the southeastern end of the island. A hike (it takes about three hours to do the whole trail) along this ridge reveals a facet of Hong Kong Island that many – even residents – never take the time to appreciate: the lush greenery blanketing the hillsides that slope down to the blue sea. This hiking trail – one of the

most popular in the area – offers maximum reward for minimum effort. You won't need climbing gear, but don't forget your swimsuit. The hike begins near Mount Collinson and ends at the coastal village of **Shek O** (see Beaches) on the eastern side of the island. Weather permitting, along the way you will be able to catch a glimpse of offshore islands, the Tai Tam reservoirs, the peaks of Mount Parker, Mount Butler and Violet Hill, the village of Stanley, and even the Kowloon peninsula.

After that trek, you deserve a treat. In the laid-back village of Shek O – the final step on the Dragon's Back – you'll find restaurants along with a pleasant beach where you can

Teeing Off

With lower fees and a wider selection for non-members, the golf courses in Macau and Southern China draw both residents of and visitors to Hong Kong. Southern China now boasts so many courses (more than 50), that playing is simply a case of visiting a travel agent in Hong Kong to choose among the many golf packages. Check out the China pages of online golf-package specialist **GolfnTours.com** (www.golfntours.com) for current information and to book greens fees and accommodation packages across the border from Hong Kong. Many of these courses are designed by international golf stars and celebrated golf-course architects; Mission Hills in Shenzhen, part of a luxury resort, is reputed to be one of the best.

MUST DO

Spectator Sports

If you prefer to watch, Hong Kong hosts a number of sports tournaments. **The Hong Kong Sevens** international rugby tournament takes place in March or April, while the premiere golf event, the **Hong Kong Open Golf Championships**, are held in December in Fanling (*New Territories*). Horse racing, of course, is the island's most beloved spectator sport; be sure to catch a race at the Happy Valley or Sha Tin tracks if your time permits (*see Horse Racing*).

Dragon's Back Trail

© Alex Havret/Apa Publications

take a refreshing dip. A 20-minute walk from Shek O, **Big Wave Bay** (*see Beaches*) is a surfing hot spot.

Golf

With flat land a scarcity in Hong Kong, private golf clubs charge a fortune for a membership. But, thanks to a public course and non-membership policies at a couple of private clubs, golf is accessible to island visitors.

The territory's only public course is located on the scenic island of **Kau Sai Chau** (*www.kscgolf.com*), just off Sai Kung's promenade, where there is a designated ferry pier for players to catch a shuttle boat. Bookings can be made online.

The **Hong Kong Golf Club** in Fanling in the New Territories

(2670 1211; www.hkgolfclub.org) welcomes visitors from Monday to Friday on its course.

And the **Clearwater Bay Golf & Country Club** *(2791 3388; www.cwbgolf.org)* in the New Territories opens its greens to non-members two days per week. On Lantau Island, **Discovery Bay Golf Club** *(2791 338; www.cwb golf.org)* welcomes visitors three days a week.

Hong Kong Geopark

Tsiu Hang, Sai Kung; from Diamond Hill or Choi Hung MTR, take bus no. 92 to Sai Kung, get off at Pak Kong bus stop and follow signs to the Visitor Centre. www.geopark.gov.hk.

Recently established, Hong Kong's designated Geopark strives to conserve unique landforms, landscapes and associated wildlife in eight selected areas of the New Territories. All are on remote islands, several of which have unusual dramatic rock formations created by volcanic activity millennia ago. You can learn all about the project in the **Geopark Visitor Centre** at the Lions Nature Education Centre *(open year-round Wed–Mon 9:30am–4:30pm)*. Consult the park's website for advice on how best to visit the various parts of the Geopark.

THE GREAT OUTDOORS

HORSE RACING

The British introduced the sport of horse racing to the island in the mid-19C, and today watching a race is one of the most exciting ways to spend a few hours in Hong Kong – whether you are genuinely interested in horses galloping around a track or not. If you are, you'll be awed by the caliber of the international racehorses and jockeys that compete here. The fact that racing is the only legal form of gambling (other than the lottery) in Hong Kong helps account for its popularity. Admission costs for the public stands are low, and private boxes are also reasonable compared to those in other countries. The **Hong Kong Tourist Board** *(www.hktb.com)* offers racing packages that allow access to some otherwise restricted parts of the course. Affordable food and beverages are available from concessions on the grounds.

Horse Racing is an obsession for some attendees, and a visit to one of the city's two tracks proves an enlightening sociological experience. Hong Kongers, normally very controlled emotionally, behave differently trackside; you'll hear loud whoops of joy and cries of despair as the winners pass the finishing line. Between races, serious fans bury themselves in the newspaper racing pages before placing their last-minute wagers. Check the Hong Kong Jockey Club's website *(www.hkjc.com)* for more information.

🐎 Happy Valley Racecourse

2 Sports Rd., Happy Valley, Hong Kong Island. MTR: Causeway Bay; or take the tram to the Happy Valley terminus. Races usually held Sept–Jun Wed 7:15pm–9:15pm. 2895 1523. www.happyvalley racecourse.com.

Opened in 1846 and built on once-swampy reclaimed land, Happy Valley Racecourse is the oldest track in Asia outside Mainland China. Today the track offers state-of-the-art computerized betting with the races broadcast live on huge screens. Evening races are an awesome sight, with floodlights illuminating the track – which is

Happy Valley Racecourse

Hong Kong Tourism Board

surrounded by a twinkling ring of
residential towers – and stands full
of enthusiastic fans.
For more about the history of
racing, stop by the **Hong Kong
Racing Museum** at the Hong Kong
Jockey Club *(2/F Happy Valley
Stand; open Tue–Sun 10am–5pm;
2966-8065; www.hkjc.com)*.
Exhibits here detail the sport of
horse racing in Hong Kong since its
inception in the 19C to the present
– and the museum offers a great
view of the track.

Sha Tin Racecourse

*Tai Po Rd., Sha Tin, New Territories.
MTR: Racecourse. Races usually
held Sun afternoons (times vary)
Sept–Jun. 2695-6223.
www.sha-tin.com.*

Sha Tin's newer (1978) track, the
larger of the two with a capacity
of 85,000 spectators and a
retractable roof, is most often used
for Sunday races. The buildings
surrounding the race track in this
New Territories town are low-rise
compared to the towers that
frame Happy Valley.

Neither course compares to Ascot
or Aintree; Happy Valley and Sha
Tin are distinct to Hong Kong, and
a visit to either one is memorable.
The biggest race at Sha Tin, the
internationally renowned **Hong
Kong Derby**, takes place in March
and runs only four-year-olds.
In the middle of the track, 20-acre
Penfold Park has a lake that
attracts many species of birds.
If you've got little ones with you,
the park makes a nice place to let
them run off some steam *(closed
Mon and on race days)*.

HORSE RACING

BEACHES

Hong Kong, unbeknownst to many, is home to a number of lovely beaches. Those on Hong Kong Island, such as **Deep Water Bay**★ and **Repulse Bay**★ draw the biggest crowds since they are convenient to reach by bus. Though slightly farther away, **Stanley**'s beaches can also get cramped. Beaches on **Clearwater Bay**★ *(see New Territories)* are popular, but wide enough so you can get some personal space. On the south side of Hong Kong Island, Shek O and Big Wave Bay have fewer visitors, particularly on weekdays. If you really want to escape crowds, head for one of the **outlying islands** *(see Excursions)*. Or for arguably the most stunning beach – and a quieter one – try **Big Wave Bay** in the New Territories.

🏖 Deep Water Bay★

South coast of Hong Hong Island. Buses 6, 6A, and 260 from Exchange Square, Central.

First stop on the bus ride to Repulse Bay and Stanley, Deep Water Bay is one of the best beaches in Hong Kong. Although small, this site is popular with the locals – and little-known to tourists. A pedestrian walkway connects Deep Water Bay to its neighbor, Repulse Bay.

Repulse Bay★

South coast of Hong Hong Island. Buses 6, 6A, and 260 from Exchange Square, Central.

This wide, crescent-shaped beach, one of the longest on the island, packs on the crowds when it's hot and sunny. Up until the 1970s,

Repulse Bay Beach

© Stelya/Dreamstime.com

Repulse Bay was almost wild. Since then, developers have realized its potential, and enclosed the bay in a ring of concrete. Hong Kong's most popular beach, however, remains agreeable, even if the water is not always crystal-clear. The hub of the social scene here was once the Repulse Bay Hotel *(see sidebar, below)*, which was torn down in 1982. A modern replica – The Repulse Bay – now stands

Historic Repulse Bay Hotel

Known for its striking perch above the bay, its impeccable service and its fine cuisine, the Repulse Bay Hotel reigned as one of Hong Kong's premiere accommodations for 62 years. During its heyday, the hotel was favored by royalty and glitterati such as Crown Prince Juan Carlos of Spain, actor Marlon Brando, and writer George Bernard Shaw. The hotel, which was once the place to go to the beach on weekends, was immortalized in the 1955 Hollywood film *Love Is A Many Splendoured Thing*.

MUST DO

The Beachy Life on Lamma Island

Far from the skyscrapers of Hong Kong, Lamma is easily reached in 30 minutes by boat from Outlying Ferry Pier Number 4 in Central. Beaches near both the island's public ferry terminals include Hung Shing Ye (with lifeguards, showers and changing rooms), a 25-minute walk from Ying Shue Wan pier, and excellent **Lo Lo Shing★**, a 10-minute walk from Sok Kwu Wan ferry pier. Start or end a visit to a Lamma beach at one of the area's fine seafood restaurants.

on the site and houses a couple of good, if pricey, restaurants.

Silvermine Bay Beach★

Mui Wo, Lantau Island. Outlying Ferry Pier Number 6, Central Piers. MTR: Tung Chau.

Ringed by green mountains, the long stretch of powdery sand bordering the South China Sea at Silvermine Bay Beach has a roped-off, attended swimming area. It also has the extra appeal of being backed by low-rise Mui Wo Village, so there are plenty of restaurants, cafés and bars to enjoy before or after baking on the sand.

Shek O Beaches

South coast of Hong Kong Island. MTR: Shau Kei Wan; then take bus no. 9 or a taxi.

Sheltered by two remote headlands on the southeastern end of Hong Kong Island, the beach off the village of Shek O is backed by open-fronted restaurants and bars. A 20-minute walk along the headland leads to less crowded **Big Wave Bay**, known for its sizeable breakers. Amenities here are limited, but this doesn't dissuade members of Hong Kong's surfing community who seek out the bay's big waves here.

Stanley Beaches

Buses 6, 6A, 6X and 260 from Exchange Square, Central.

Known more for its market, cafés and bars, Stanley also offers beaches on both sides of its peninsula. Both **Stanley Main Beach** on the east side and **St. Stephen's Beach** on the west boast long stretches of sand that attract swimmers and water- and jet-skiers. These beaches also have netted swimming areas to protect swimmers from sharks.

Tai Long Wan Beach

Sai Kung East Country Park, on the Sai Kung Peninsula. MTR: Diamond Hill or Choi Hung MTR. From the station, take bus no. 92 to Sai Kung and bus no. 94 to Wong Shek Pier; then take a speedboat to Chek Keng. Or take a taxi from the MTR station to Wong Shek Pier.

Why take the trek to get here? To see what is said to be Hong Kong's most unspoiled and dramatic beach: a sparkling blue-green bay with a backdrop of rugged headlands. Tai Long Wan means "Big Wave Bay" – not to be confused with the one on Hong Kong Island – and indeed surfers are drawn to the swells here.

BEACHES

107

THEME PARKS

Got kids in tow? Make a beeline for one of Hong Kong's two theme parks. Between the fishy denizens and rides at Ocean Park and the myriad attractions of Hong Kong Disneyland, a good time is guaranteed for the whole family.

Hong Kong Disneyland★★

Sunny Bay, Lantau Island.
MTR: Disneyland Resort.
Open Mon–Fri 10:30am–8:30pm, weekends and holidays 10am– 9pm. HK$350 (HK$250/children). park.hongkongdisneyland.com.

Launched in 2005, Hong Kong Disneyland (which has its own special-edition MTR train with Mickey Mouse-head-shaped windows) is divided into four areas: **Tomorrowland**, **Fantasyland**, **Adventureland** and **Main Street USA**. An additional area, **Toy Story Land**, is scheduled to open by the end of 2011.

Hong Kong Disneyland

© Pindiyath100/Dreamstime.com

Park Highlights

The **Space Mountain** ride may not be as tall as some in the world but it's a spine-tingler of a roller-coaster. This coaster hurtles you up and down in the dark, and every corner comes as a surprise. Younger children will enjoy joining **Buzz Lightyear** to shoot lasers at evil aliens; riding one of Disney's **Cars** characters on a special track; and taking a cruise down an Amazon-like river, peppered with Disney's signature audio-animatronic animals that pop up when you least expect them. Besides the rides, there are daily parades; a vibrant **Lion King** performance in a custom-built theater; and, of course, the chance to meet Disney characters as you walk through the park.

The new, gravity-defying **Flights of Fantasy Parade** – which took 18 months to develop – dazzles with miniature hot-air balloons soaring up to 12m/40ft in the air.

Touring Tip

Note that lines can be long for some rides at peak times, so consider buying a special **Star Pass** that allows you to get quick access to the most popular rides and attractions (*available online for HK$198*). It's easy to spend a full day at the park; if you think you might like to stay longer – there are two hotels in the park: **Hong Kong Disneyland Hotel** and **Disney's Hollywood Hotel** (*see Hotels*).

MUST DO

Rainforest Awareness

Educational exhibits and experiences are things that **Ocean Park** has always focused on, in addition to its amusement rides. In June 2011, the park opened a new zone called **RainForest**. Its Discovery Trail showcases and explains the habitat of more than 1,000 creatures, including some 70 species of fish, mammals, birds and insects. Catch the antics of the Pygmy Marmoset, the world's smallest monkey; and see the Hercules beetle, the world's strongest animal – capable of lifting an unprecedented 850 times its own body weight. Marvel or grimace at the world's largest rodent, the Capybara; and the largest freshwater fish, the Arapaima, from South America.

⛲ Ocean Park★

Ocean Park Rd. (off Wong Chuk Hang Rd.), Aberdeen, Hong Kong Island. MTR: Admiralty, then express bus no. 629 to Ocean Park. Open daily 9:30am–8pm. HK$280 (HK$140/child age 3-11). 3923 2323. www.oceanpark.com.hk.

Part theme park, part aquarium, this sight lets you choose between thrilling rides and educational marine displays. Located on the island's south shore, the park comprises two different areas: the lowland Waterfront and the Summit on the headlands above. The two parts of the park are connected by **cable car** and funicular railway. If the cable car line is too long, take the Ocean Express train. Its ceiling is fitted with LED panels that simulate an underwater journey as you go.

The Waterfront

Housed in a giant multilevel tank, a layered interpretation of the ecosystem of coastal Hong Kong fills the three-story **Grand Aquarium**. From viewpoints above and below the tank, you can admire the graceful flight of stingrays, sharks, sea turtles and some 400 species of fish. Near the entrance, the **HKJC Giant Panda**

Panda Habitat, Ocean Park
© Florent Bonnefoy/Michelin

Habitat is home to four members of this endangered species. An An and Jia Jia were given to Hong Kong by the central government in 1999 to celebrate the transfer of sovereignty. They were joined by Le Le and Ying Ying in 2007 on the 10-year anniversary of the transfer. A new extravaganza held at closing time sparks the night with water displays, pyrotechnics, music and animation at **Aqua City Lagoon**.

The Summit

Aquatic and bird shows are staged in the Summit's **Ocean Theatre** (*check online for schedules*). You'll find the thrill rides here too, including two rollercoasters, a Raging River, a Ferris wheel, and **The Flash**, which spins riders around at dizzying speeds of 60km/hr (37mi/hr).

FAMILY FUN

Whether you're taking the family on a tram ride to the top of Victoria Peak★★★, or a trip to Hong Kong Disneyland, this region has plenty to engage the interest of children. In recent years, some of the territory's museums have been revamped with interactive exhibits that appeal especially to children. This applies particularly to the Science Museum and the Museum of History★★★ *(see Museums)***, both of which have spared no expense with their hands-on displays**.

Victoria Peak★★★

The lower terminus is on Garden Road, opposite St. John's Cathedral. Funicular railway: leaves every 10–15min from 7am–midnight. HK\$40 round-trip. Or take bus no. 15 from Exchange Square in Central. www.thepeak. com.hk.

One of Hong Kong's most popular attractions, The Peak, as it's now known (*see Regions/Hong Kong Island North*), is accessible via the **Peak Tram**, a funicular railway that began operation in 1888 (no worries – it has been modernized since then).

As the tram climbs up the steep mountain on its seven-minute trip, you'll have breathtaking views of the island. From the tram station at the top, a short walk up Mount Austin Road leads to a large **playground**. Another

easy walk, a loop trail circles the peak, revealing lush green hillsides sloping down to the sea. At **Madame Tussaud's** museum, both kids and adults will delight in the wax renditions of kung fu

Victoria Peak

Hong Kong Tourism Board

Walk Around An Island

Outlying Ferry Pier No. 6, Central Piers, Central, Hong Kong. MTR: Central.
Imagine the satisfaction a child will feel after having circumnavigated an entire island. On tiny **Peng Chau** island (*1km²/0.38sq mi; see Excursions/ Outlying Islands*) you can easily do this. The island's fishing harbor, morning fish market, 200-year-old **Tin Hau Temple**, and port village with its warren of small lanes reveal many aspects of traditional Hong Kong rural life. These are all best discovered on an easy one-hour walk through the village and surrounding hills. Follow the signs for the **Family Trail**, and afterwards, stop for some authentic Chinese food in one of the village's restaurants.

MUST DO

stars, Hollywood movie actors and famous sports figures *(2849 6966; www.madamtussauds.com/ hongkong; open daily 10am– 10pm; HK$160, HK$90/child).*

Hong Kong Disneyland★★

Sunny Bay, Lantau Island. MTR: Disneyland Resort. Open Mon–Fri 10:30am–8:30pm, weekends and holidays 10am– 9pm. HK$350 (HK$250/child). park. hongkongdisneyland.com. See Theme Parks.

Disney magic invades the territory at this 22ha/55-acre theme park, where Mickey, Minnie and a host of other Disney characters come to life.

Hong Kong Zoological and Botanical Gardens★

Albany Rd., Central, Hong Kong Island. MTR: Central. Open year- round daily 6am–7pm (10pm for Fountain Terrace). 2530 0154. www.lcsd.gov.hk/parks. See Parks and Gardens.

Set on the northern slope of Victoria Peak, this site devotes roughly half of its landscaped 5ha/13acres to a zoo. The gardens are divided into two parts, the Old Garden on the east side and the New Garden to the west. The majority of the zoo's mammals and reptiles are kept in the New Garden. Highlights include a host of monkeys, and reptiles such as Chinese alligators and Burmese pythons. Find a children's playground and aviaries alive with some 400 birds in the Old Garden.

Ocean Park

© Alex Havret/Apa Publications

Ocean Park★

Ocean Park Rd. (off Wong Chuk Hang Rd.), Aberdeen, Hong Kong Island. MTR: Admiralty, then express bus no. 629 to Ocean Park. 3923 2323. www.oceanpark. com.hk. See Theme Parks.

Since Hong Kong Disneyland opened, this theme park/aquarium has ploughed a lot of funds into making itself a serious contender for the attention of both local and visiting patrons.

A Day at the Beach

What's more fun than a day at the beach? Hong Kong has several good sandy stretches *(see Beaches)*, many with amenities such as lifeguards and changing facilities. Choice vary from close-in – and more crowded – beaches to sands that are more remote and tranquil. Before you go, stop at a local pharmacy and pick up some high- factor sunscreen.

FAMILY FUN

Hong Kong Maritime Museum

Murray House, Stanley Plaza, Stanley, Hong Kong Island. Take bus numbers 6, 6A and 260 from Exchange Square Terminus in Central. Open Tue–Sun 10am–6pm. HK$20, HK$10/child. 2813 2322. www.hkmaritimemuseum.org.

Located inside 19C Murray House, this museum chronicles how Hong Kong's maritime activities transformed what was once a handful of sleepy fishing villages into the bustling port you see today. In the museum, youngsters will discover the story of Hong Kong's maritime prowess through ship models, display boards and a mock-up bridge of a ship that you can "sail" through a virtual rendition of Victoria Harbour. Displays also show how China, Asia and the West developed ships for all kinds of uses, including exploration, trade and war.

Hong Kong Science Museum

2 Science Museum Rd., Tsim Sha Tsui, Kowloon. MTR: Tsim Sha Tsui. Open Mon–Wed & Fri 1pm–9pm, Sat, Sun & holidays 10am–9pm. HK$25, HK$12.50/ child (free Wed). 2732 3232. www.hk.science. museum.

This museum proves that science can be fun and accessible – especially to small children. Visitors here take a hands-on approach to learning about the basic principles of everyday science. Some 500 exhibits fill 16 galleries in the permanent exhibition area. One must-see highlight, the four-story-tall **Energy Machine** is the largest of its kind in the world. Set it in motion and you'll see a continuous stream of balls roll along tracks within and between the machine's twin towers.

The **hall of mirrors** is another winner with the young at heart; and there are always well-curated temporary exhibitions.

In the **Childrens Gallery**, young visitors can learn about surface tension by watching the colorful bubbles and soapy film that they make themselves with bubble hoops. They can also push buttons to move cone-shaped train wheels, with outer rims smaller than the inner one, to demonstrate what prevents trains from derailing.

Hong Kong Space Museum

10 Salisbury Rd., Tsim Sha Tsui, Kowloon. MTR: Tsim Sha Tsui. Open Mon & Wed–Fri 1pm–9pm, Sat, Sun & holidays 10am–9pm. Closed Tue. HK$10, HK$5/child. Additional fee for Omnimax shows. 2721 0226. www.hk.space.museum.

This museum thrills young visitors with its interactive installations and real astronaut uniforms. It's quite small, so you'll be hard-pressed to occupy the kids for more than about 45 minutes here.

Hong Kong Space Museum

Hong Kong Tourism Board

MUST DO

Menus for the Younger Set

Very few Hong Kong restaurants serve children's portions; in Asia, it's more common for a group of diners to all share whatever dishes are ordered. However, in some Chinese restaurants and other eateries, smaller sizes of the listed dishes are available. Whether kids' portions are listed on the menu or not, it never hurts to ask. So if you are traveling with small frys who are picky eaters, this may give you more menu flexibility. Western-style restaurants in the middle-to-high price range often do offer kids' menus.

For more fun, check out the Sky Show and the Omnimax films screened in the **Space Theatre** (*check online or at admission desk for showtimes*) to the rumblings of surround-sound.

Sheung Yiu Family Walk

Pak Tam Chung Nature Trail, Sai Kung, New Territories. MTR: Diamond Hill or Choi Hung, then take bus no. 92 to Sai Kung. From Sai Kung, take bus no. 94 to Pak Tam Chung; walk for 5min to the starting point at Renaissance Bridge on Tai Mong Tsai Rd. (route is marked with signs). 2792 7365. www.afcd.gov.hk.

Situated within the vast 4,477ha/ 11,060-acre **Sai Kung East Country Park**, the **Sheung Yiu Family Walk** follows a flat and lush circular route (*1km/0.6mi*) that takes about an hour to traverse (the trail begins near the park's visitor center). Along the way, you'll passing labeled sub-tropical plants and trees, and other unlabeled vegetation including several types of tall grasses. Also on this easy shaded trail is the **Sheung Yiu Folk Museum** (*see Chinese Heritage Sites*), a time capsule of rural 19C Southern Chinese village life that is sure to interest all ages.

Star Ferry Harbor Tour

Boats depart from the Star Ferry Pier in Central. Ferries runs between Central and Tsim Sha Tsui daily 6:30am–11:30pm, at 10min intervals. HK$2.50 for upper deck, HK$2 for lower deck. 2367 7065. www.starferry.com.hk.
See Theme Tours.

Both kids and adults will enjoy a harbor tour on these clunky yet charismatic wooden-decked boats.

Take the Tram

HK$2 for adults; pay as you exit. 2548 7102. www.hktramways.com.
See Theme Tours.

Trundling along Hong Kong Island's north shore in a 50- to 100-year-old iron tram is a truly memorable experience – and it's guaranteed to provide fun for the whole family.

Hong Kong Tourism Board

Double-decker Tram

FAMILY FUN

PERFORMING ARTS

While Hong Kong may not project its interest globally, performing arts are a long-established part of the social fabric here. Reflecting the true nature of the place itself, Hong Kong stages a good mix of Chinese and non-Chinese productions. The former include various styles of Chinese Opera, as well as modern drama and musicals in Cantonese. Larger venues offer English-language subtitles, projected on screens to the side of the stage. There's a regular season of classical concert and dance performances, and international bands take the stage now and then too.

Several arts festivals are now held annually; the largest ones are the Hong Kong Arts Festival, City Fringe Festival, Le French May, Italian Quality and Lifestyle and New Vision Arts Festival *(see Calendar of Events)*. The best one-stop websites for an overview of area performances are: www.lcsd.gov.hk and www.hkticketing.com.

PERFORMING ARTS VENUES

Hong Kong Academy for Performing Arts

*HKAPA, 1 Gloucester Rd., Wan Chai, Hong Kong Island. **MTR: Wan Chai.** Box office open Mon–Sat noon–6pm. 2584 8500. www.hkapa.edu.*

Set on the edge of Victoria Harbor in Wan Chai, the HKAPA enjoys a stellar reputation in Asia and is the grooming ground for Hong Kong and regional stars-in-the-making in dance, drama, pop and other musical genres, radio, television and film, as well as choreographers, directors and producers.

Hong Kong Arts Centre

*HKAC, 2 Harbour Rd., Wan Chai, Hong Kong Island. **MTR: Wan Chai.** Box office open Mon–Sat noon–6pm. 2582 0200. www.hkac.org.hk.*

Next door to the Hong Kong Academy for the Performing Arts, the Hong Kong Arts Centre devotes itself to promoting contemporary arts and culture.

Kowloon Clock Tower

A few meters from the Hong Kong Cultural Centre, you can see the 1915 red brick and granite clock tower slightly hidden in the shadow of surrounding modern buildings. The tower is all that remains of the Kowloon train station that was demolished in 1978 in favor of seafront development. Originally, the station was meant to be the starting point for a railroad connecting Hong Kong to Europe through Beijing, Mongolia and Moscow. But it apparently didn't merit saving in the face of the area's burgeoning development. The Hong Kong Section of the Kowloon-Canton Railway opened in 1910, and the terminus in Tsim Sha Tsui was completed in 1915. Though now dwarfed by modern structures, the 44m/144ft-high clock tower is a local landmark. Its cupola is crowned with a 7m/23ft lightning rod.

MUST DO

Hong Kong Cultural Centre

© Ming Yin Tang/Dreamstime.com

Its two theaters produce a mixture of performances, drama and film among them.

Hong Kong City Hall

5 Edinburgh Place, Central. MTR: Central. Box office open 10am–9.30pm.2921 2840. www.cityhall.gov.hk.

Hidden in the middle of Central's business district, across the street from Statue Square, City Hall maintains a busy annual schedule in its two performance spaces. Concerts and musicals by local and international companies are held in the concert hall, while the theater hosts plays and films.

Hong Kong Cultural Centre

10 Salisbury Rd., Tsim Sha Tsui, Kowloon. MTR: Tsim Sha Tsui. Open year-round daily 9am–11pm. 2734 9009. www.lcsd.gov.hk.

An enormous low building facing Victoria Harbour, the Cultural Centre has been criticized for its pink-tiled windowless façade and peculiar angled shape. Still, it represents a courageous effort to transform Hong Kong into one of the cultural and artistic capitals of Asia. The Centre includes three major performing spaces – the Concert Hall, the Grand Theatre, and the small Studio Theatre – and is renowned for the exceptional quality of its performances.

Treat yourself to a musical performance in the oval, two-tiered **Concert Hall**. With more than 2,000 seats in the round, the hall boasts world-class acoustics and is home to a striking 8,000-pipe **Austrian organ**, one of the largest in the world.

If you aren't lucky enough to be able to attend a production, you can always take a guided tour to get a sense of the interior (*by reservation; HK$10*). Performances are at their most prolific during the annual Hong Kong Arts Festival, in February and March, when international and local productions are held all over town. The Centre's lobby is home to exhibitions of two-dimensional art – sometimes works by professionals, other times works by area high school or college students.

PERFORMING ARTS

Fringe Club

2 Lower Albert Rd., Central.
MTR: Central. Box office open
noon–10pm. 2521 7251.
www.hkfringeclub.com.

With its small bars, cafes and galleries, The Fringe Club attracts an artsy crowd who favor the less mainstream performances staged here. A former cold-storage warehouse, the colonial-era structure holds two intimate theaters, and the ground-floor bar has a tiny stage where small bands play. After a performance, enjoy a cocktail and light fare in the pleasant rooftop garden.

PRODUCTION COMPANIES

Chung Ying Theatre Company

Various venues. 2521 6628.
www.chungying.com.

Launched with support from the British Council in 1979, Chung Ying Theatre Company is now funded by the government and numbers among the leading professional theater companies in Hong Kong. It stages energetic English- and Chinese-language productions, mostly drama, the latter with projected English subtitles.

Hong Kong Ballet

Various venues. 2105 9724.
www.hkballet.com.

More than three decades old, and performing regularly at some of the best theaters in town, the Hong Kong Ballet is considered one of the premier classical ballet companies in Asia. As such, its troupe regularly includes acclaimed dancers from Mainland China and Japan. Its repertoire takes in classics such as *Swan Lake* and *The Nutcracker* as well as original works by local choreographers.

Hong Kong Chinese Orchestra

Various venues. 3185-1600.
www.hkco.org.

One of the largest Chinese orchestras in the world, the 58-piece HKCO consists of four

Chinese Opera

With all its bright faces, silk costumes, and uniquely intoned vocals over a one-of-a-kind orchestra, Chinese Opera is alive and well in Hong Kong. And it has a large audience – albeit one with an average age hovering around 60. As in early Western stage shows, performers seemingly of one gender are often actually the opposite sex. Scripts are mostly the same ones that have been used for generations, and the movements and high-pitched vocals are all highly stylized and accompanied by lively percussion and wind instruments. Costume and make-up colors symbolize particular character traits in the story line.

© A. Bossler/fotolia.com

sections: bowed strings, plucked strings, wind and percussion.
The group finds it roots in Chinese cultural heritage, although they do also experiment with full-scale contemporary works.
With some 100 members, HKCO's growth in recent years reflects the public's continuous interest in learning about and listening to classical Chinese music.
The orchestra organizes more than 100 regular and outreach concerts each year.

Hong Kong Dance Company

Various venues. 3103 1888.
www.hkdance.com.

Devoted to promoting Chinese dance since 1981, the HKDC wins raves for its repertoire, which encompasses traditional and folk dances as well as original dance productions with both traditional Chinese and more modern Hong Kong themes.
One of the company's proudest moments was performing during the Beijing Olympics of 2008 in the Chinese capital. The group, which regularly gives free performances, includes a children's troupe.

Hong Kong Philharmonic Orchestra

Various venues. 2734 9009.
www.hkpo.com.

One of Asia's leading orchestras, the Hong Kong Philharmonic has performed for more than a century. Its international musicians attract world-class collaborations on stage. HKPO annually touches the lives of more than 200,000 music lovers through some 150

performances. If you have a chance, try to catch one of their concerts at either the City Hall Theatre or at the Cultural Centre Concert Hall.

Hong Kong Players

Various venues.
www.hongkongplayers.com.

This community theater group dates back to 1844, when it was founded as the Hong Kong Amateur Dramatic Society, making it the longest-running theater group on the island. In the group's early days, productions by Noel Coward and other British playwrights were its mainstay; today the troupe is multicultural and so is its repertoire.

Hong Kong Repertory Theatre

Various venues. 3103 5930.
www.hkrep.com.

Founded in 1977, the Hong Kong Rep – as it is locally known – is the largest professional theater company of its kind in Hong Kong. The non-profit organization claims a large team of professional actors, who often collaborate with playwrights and artistic directors of different backgrounds.
This results in a diverse array of productions – in Chinese and English – many of which are held at the Hong Kong City Hall Theatre.

PERFORMING ARTS

SHOPPING

In Hong Kong, shopping is an obsession. You can easily spend a half-day or more just in the malls, your feet never touching the street as you stroll between the interconnecting centers. On Hong Kong Island, you'll find some of the world's glitziest showrooms; Landmark, IFC Mall and Pacific Place are the swankiest. **Canton Road** in Tsim Sha Tsui, Kowloon offers a similar experience, though shops tend to be more affordable here. This same neighborhood has recently become home to the two high-tech malls, i-Square and K11.

Nathan Road★★★, once a popular shopping destination, doesn't offer as much in the way of retail excitement these days. Hong Kong's electronics shops are not what they once were either, though two chain stores, **Fortress** (www.fortress.com.hk) and **Broadway** (www.ibroadway.com.hk) – found all over the city – are worth a stop. Here, by category, are some of the island's best places to shop.

ANTIQUES

Most antique shops cluster together along **Hollywood Road★★** in the Central district on Hong Kong Island. (The farther west you walk away from Central on this road, the more reasonable the prices become.) The two dealers listed here have a good reputation for selling high-quality antiques.

🔥 Arch Angel Antiques

53-55 Hollywood Rd., Central. MTR: Central. Open daily 9:30am–6:30pm. 2851 6848.

Arch Angel offers a good selection of mostly Chinese and some Southeast Asian antiques. Expect competent personnel and original quality pieces.

Honeychurch Antiques

29 Hollywood Rd., Central. MTR: Central. Open Mon–Sat 10am–6pm. 2543 2433. www.honeychurch.com.

This institution on Hollywood Road sells rare antiques from all over Asia, and is known for its reliability. Expect high prices in keeping with the quality of the antiques.

Herbs and Potions

Traditional pharmacies offering the ingredients used in Chinese medicine are concentrated in Sheung Wan (Hong Kong Island) around Queen's Road and Bonham Strand (MTR: Sheung Wan). The shelves of the shops in this area display stag horns, dried mussels, all types of flowers and other, more unusual ingredients that are used to make healing potions in Traditional Chinese Medicine, or TCM (*see Regions/Hong Kong Island North*). The most famous Chinese pharmacy is **Beijing Tong Ren Tang** (*33 Queen's Rd., Central; 2868 0609*) on Hong Kong Island. Another authentic shop is Shue Tso Tong (*74 Wan Chai Rd., Wan Chai, Hong Kong Island; MTR: Wan Chai; 2573 2380*); the plants sold there are guaranteed to be free of pesticides.

MUST DO

Art Shopping, Hollywood Road

Hong Kong Tourism Board

ART GALLERIES

Concentrated in SoHo (upper Central), and on and around Hollywood Road and Wyndham Street, art galleries often intermingle with antique shops. You will also find them between Central and Causeway Bay, and in Tsim Sha Tsui, in Kowloon.

Asia Fine Art

Sik On St., 99 Queen's Rd. East, Wan Chai, Hong Kong Island. **MTR: Wan Chai.** *Open daily 10:30am–6:30pm. 2522 0405. www.asia-fineart.com.*

The owners of this shop have been collecting fine art from Vietnam and China for some 30 years. Promoting emerging artists from across Asia, the fine-art gallery holds a remarkable collection of works and sponsors more than 20 different exhibitions each year.

Gallery by the Harbour

Ocean Centre, Shop 207, Level 2, Harbour City, Tsim Sha Tsui, Kowloon. Open daily 11am–9pm. **MTR: Wan Chai.** *www.harbour city.com.hk.*

Works by local, Asian, and occasionally, international artists rotate in this bright space in Ocean Centre mall.

Schoeni Art Gallery

Two Central locations: 21-31 Old Bailey St. (2869 8802) and 27 Hollywood Rd. (2542 3143) Hong Kong Island. **MTR: Central.** *Open Mon–Sat 10:30am–6:30pm.*

The original and larger gallery on Old Bailey Street was one of the first (1992) to show Chinese Avant-Garde, Neo-Realism and Pop Art works by artists from Mainland China. Schoeni offers contemporary oil paintings and prints by well-known PRC artists, and prices are quite high.

10 Chancery Lane Gallery

10 Chancery Lane, off Old Bailey St., Central. **MTR: Central.** *Open Mon–Fri 11am–7pm, Sat 11:30am–6pm. 2810 0065. www.10chancerylanegallery.com.*

Tucked away behind the heritage Central Police Station, this SoHo gallery displays works in a variety of media by artists from Hong Kong, Mainland China, Vietnam and other parts of Asia.

Zee Stone Gallery

1 Hollywood Rd., Central. **MTR: Central.** *Mon–Sat 10am–6:30pm, Sun & holidays 1pm–5pm. 2810 5895. www.zeestone.com.*

Located in G/F Chinachem Hollywood Centre, Zee Stone specializes in Mainland China artists working in both Chinese ink on paper and in oil on canvas. The gallery also deals in Chinese antiques, which you'll need to ask about, as these pieces are not normally on display.

SHOPPING

MALLS AND DEPARTMENT STORES

Shops in Hong Kong's malls are generally open from 10am–9pm. All the malls mentioned here contain numerous restaurants and smaller eateries, convenient for when you need a break from rifling through merchandise.

⚜ Elements

1 Austin Rd. West, Jordan, Kowloon. MTR: Jordan. 2735 5234. www.elementshongkong.com.

Divided into five areas based on the five elements of nature (metal, wood, wind, fire and water), airy Elements mall is linked to the Kowloon MTR and Airport Express stations. Contemporary sculptures punctuate the mall, which feels more spacious than most malls, owing to the fact that its developers did not pack retail outlets into every square inch. Shops mix designer fashion, sporting goods, products for the home and electronics; there's even an ice rink on the ground floor and a terrace garden with bars and cafés.

G.O.D.

Leighton Centre, Sharp St. East, Causeway Bay, Hong Kong Island. MTR: Causeway Bay. Open daily noon–10pm. 2881 8196. www.god.com.hk.

A cross between a shop and a Hong Kong pop-culture museum, this lifestyle store sports a witty name – an acronym for Goods of Desire – and features edgy Hong Kong-designed home furnishings and funky casual clothing, handbags and accessories that bear contemporary Chinese motifs. G.O.D. has several branches around Hong Kong.

Harbour City

3-27 Canton Rd., Tsim Sha Tsui, Kowloon. MTR: Tsim Sha Tsui. 2118 8666. www.harbourcity.com.hk.

Only a few steps away from the debarkation area of the Tsim Sha Tsui Star Ferry, this immense space – one of the largest malls in Tsim Sha Tsui – comprises four shopping zones and more than 700 stores. Offerings range from local arts and crafts to Louis Vuitton handbags.

Harbour City Mall

Hong Kong Tourism Board

MUST DO

IFC Mall

1 Harbour View St., Central.
MTR: Central. 2295 3308.
www.ifc.com.hk.

On the edge of Central, IFC enjoys a stunning harbor backdrop. Containing more than 200 stores, the mall stands on land that was reclaimed only a few years ago and is home to some of Hong Kong's top designer boutiques and ritziest restaurants.

Island Beverly Centre

1 Great George St., Causeway Bay, Hong Kong Island.
MTR: Causeway Bay.

Hong Kong's mecca for the young and trendy set, this warren of tiny boutiques displays hip clothing, footwear and accessories from both local and overseas labels.

i-Square

iSquare; 63 Nathan Rd., Tsim Sha Tsui, Kowloon. MTR: Tsim Sha Tsui. 3665 3333. www.isquare.hk.

State-of-the-art in its high-tech minimalist design, i-Square incorporates long escalators and backlit highlights between its hip clothing and accessory shops. Find one of Hong Kong's best new multi-screen cinema houses on the seventh floor.

K11

18 Hanoi Rd., Tsim Sha Tsui, Kowloon. MTR station: Tsim Sha Tsui. 3118 8070. www.k11 concepts.com.

Lots of light boxes and LED panels create flashy effects on the walls of this Kowloon mall. Shops

The Landmark

© Cyril/fotolia.com

carry mostly clothing, shoes and accessories targeted at a late-teen to 30-something market. Take a break in one of the restaurants that inhabit the "gourmet tower" floors of the complex.

The Landmark

12-16 Des Voeux Rd., Central.
MTR: Central. www.centralhk.com.

The original big brand-name shopping mall in downtown Hong Kong is home to the city's one British luxury department store – **Harvey Nichols** (*15 Queen's Rd., Central; 3695 3388*) – which fills five floors with international fashion for men and women. Clothing, footwear and accessories make up the bulk of the mall's stores, with accessories and music also on tap. **Fourth Floor** restaurant draws a fashionable set for afternoon tea.

Pacific Place

88 Queensway, Admiralty, Hong Kong Island. MTR: Admiralty. 2845 4555. www.pacificplace.com.hk.

This is the mall that put the Admiralty district on the map. Sitting on top of the Admiralty

MTR station and connecting to three luxury hotels and the United Centre mall, Pacific Place is a world unto itself. Spacious halls here teem with designer-label and high-end watch shops and chic restaurants and cafés.

Sogo

555 Hennessy Rd., Causeway Bay, Hong Kong Island. MTR: Causeway Bay. Open Sun–Thu 10am–9pm, Fri–Sat 10am–10pm. 2833 8338. www.sogo.com.hk.

Smack in the middle of the busiest intersection in Causeway Bay, this Japanese department store overflows with Japanese and international wares.

Times Square

1 Matheson St., Causeway Bay, Hong Kong Island. MTR: Causeway Bay. 2295 3308. www.times square.com.hk.

This shopping and office complex was the first "vertical" mall in Hong Kong. More than 16 floors of retail offer every possible lifestyle product, plus three floors of restaurants. The plaza in front of the tower hosts the Western celebration of New Year's Eve.

Yue Hwa

301-309 Nathan Rd., Jordan, Kowloon. MTR: Jordan. Open daily 10am–10pm. 3511 2222. www.yuehwa.com.

A large seven-floor department store where you can find furniture, clothing and souvenirs of all kinds. A good selection of *cheongsams* (form-fitting Chinese dresses with a Mandarin collar, like those worn by Maggie Cheung in the 2000 film *In the Mood for Love*).

SOUVENIRS

Chinese department stores, and the markets in Stanley and Kowloon – notably the **Temple Street Night Market★★★**, and the **Ladies'** and **Jade★** markets (*see Street Markets*) are some of the best places to find clothing, silk, ornaments and tableware, and premium teas. Consider purchasing a personalized ink stamp, carved onto an engraved stone "chop" (*see Local Crafts*).

🔑 Upper Lascar Road

Central, Hong Kong Island. MTR: Central.

Known to locals as Cat Street, Upper Lascar Road was once known for its inexpensive antiques. Now this pedestrian lane has a little market filled with Mao pins, calligraphy, jewelry, statues, and other bric-a-brac – much of which is made in factories in Guangdong.

Chinese Arts & Crafts

Star House, 3 Salisbury Rd., Tsim Sha Tsui, Kowloon. MTR: Tsim Sha Tsui. 2735 4601. www.crcretail.com.

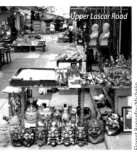

Upper Lascar Road

Florent Bonnefoy/Michelin

Tea Shops

Legend has it that tea originated in ancient China when a leaf from the *Camellia sinensis* tree feel into some water that the emperor was boiling. This beverage, which comes in green white and black varieties, has long been prized in Chinese culture. It also makes a great souvenir.

At **Fook Ming Tong Tea Shop**, you can taste the teas before you buy; the friendly staff will help you choose (*IFC Mall, 1 Harbour View St., Central; open daily 10:30am–8pm; 2295 0368; www.fookmingtong.com*). A venerable shop where tea is displayed in regal red and gold canisters, **Ki Chan Tea Co.** has been offering the finest of brews since 1942 (*174 Johnston Rd., Wan Chai; open daily 9am–7pm; 2573 0690; www.kichantea.com*).

Most visitors on a mission for a Chinese memento or gift don't leave here empty-handed. There are several Chinese emporiums across town, but this is one of the best. Clothing, furniture, ornaments, jewelery, toys, tea, table wear – it's all here.

Shanghai Tang

12 Pedder St., Pedder Building, Central. MTR: Central. Mon–Fri 10am–8pm, Sat & Sun noon–6pm. 2525 7333. www.shanghaitang.com.

Hong Kong's answer to haute couture makes for prized gifts. The founder of Shanghai Tang is a passionate upholder of his culture. His Chinese-style clothing designs are made with quality materials. Bed and bath linens, like the dishware sold here, feature a modernized Chinese style. Shanghai Tang store also offers custom-made clothing.

TAILORS

Hong Kong is a city that crawls with tailors, who are happy to craft custom-made shirts, suits and *cheongsams*, often at bargain prices. You'll find a glut of tailor shops in the area around Tsim

Sha Tsui Star Ferry Pier. Many of these, like the two listed here, are quite good and can often turn around items in one to two days, if necessary.

Linva Tailors

38 Cochrane St., Central. MTR: Central. Open daily 9:30am–6pm. 2544 2456.

Since the1960s, this shop has been making magnificent *cheongsams*. Prices vary according to the quality of the material used, from basic cotton to embroidered silk.

Sam's Tailor

94 Nathan Rd., Tsim Sha Tsui, Kowloon. MTR: Tsim Sha Tsui. Open daily 10am–7:30pm. 2367 9423. www.samstailor.com.

Probably Hong Kong's most famous tailor, Sam (whose real name is Manu) has designed clothes for the likes of President Bill Clinton and countless movie stars. You'll see evidence of this in the photographs that hang on the walls of his showroom in Burlington Arcade.

SHOPPING

STREET MARKETS

Up until a couple of decades ago, Hong Kong was home to plenty of outdoor market traders – selling their wares at regulated sites or hawking them from wheelbarrows. The government clamped down on the latter in the 1990s, stopping unauthorized vendors and issuing no more street-hawking licenses. The vigilance has been stepped up with food – both cooked and raw – too, in recent years, with many food vendors being moved into soulless utilitarian blocks.

The venues below, however, provide a good taste of Asian outdoor markets. Some, like the Flower, Jade, Goldfish and Bird markets, exist to serve the locals, but vendors here are quite accustomed to foreign visitors. At Temple Street Night Market, in particular, expect vendors to begin a sales pitch as soon as they see you coming.

With the exception of **Stanley Market** *(see Regions/Hong Kong Island South)*, which caters almost exclusively to tourists, the best markets for visitors all lie roughly in the center of Kowloon.

Temple Street Night Market★★★

Temple St., Yau Ma Tei, Kowloon. MTR: Yau Ma Tei. Open year-round daily 2pm–10pm.

People go to this surging market, which moves into full swing when the sun sets, for its bargains and atmosphere. It's a great way to experience a slice of Chinese life. In addition to the trinkets, Chinese souvenirs, and T-shirts boasting "I Love Hong Kong" or less politically correct slogans, you'll find simple tasty Cantonese fare here at one of the last of Hong Kong's *dai pai dong,* (*see sidebar, opposite*).

Temple Street Night Market

Florent Bonnefoy/Michelin

Bird Market★★

Bird Garden, at the end of Flower Market Rd., Mong Kok, Kowloon. MTR: Prince Edward. Open year-round daily 7am–8pm.

Enter the Bird Market through the archway at the end of Flower Market Road.

Now officially renamed **Yuen Po Street Bird Garden**, this place is popular with older Chinese men, who come here to "walk" their birds (in cages, of course) and possibly to add to their collection. Besides rare and not-so-rare birds, you'll see some expensive cages for sale.

Listen to bird owners crowing about the enviable qualities of their particular specimens; this market provides an insight into a favorite Chinese pastime.

Jade Market★

Kansu and Shanghai Sts., Yau Ma Tei, Kowloon. MTR: Yau Ma Tei. Open year-round daily 10am–3:30pm.

Dai Pai Dong

Hong Kong used to have numerous open-air food stalls, called *dai pai dong* in Chinese. Most of them have been removed for sanitation reasons now, but you can still find some good *dai pai dong* mixed in among the food and produce vendors at the **Graham Street Market** (*open daily 6pm–9pm*) at the bottom of Stanley Street in Central. In Yau Ma Tei, Kowloon, the *dai pai dong* selling shellfish at the **Temple Street Night Market★★★** is a favorite haunt of young Hong Kongese out on the town. These days, more and more tourists now seek them out as well. In the Mong Kok district of Kowloon, you'll uncover a handful of *dai pai dong* on **Nelson Street** and on **Fa Yuen Street**.

Two large canopies protect the treasures of the Jade Market, where you can sift through various qualities of this revered semi-precious green stone (*see Local Crafts*). Jade is the essential accessory of many Chinese people, especially in southern China. An old custom recommends that men wear a protective pendant representing Kuan Yin, the Goddess of Mercy, while women often sport a little laughing Buddha.

Flower Market

Flower Market Rd., Mong Kok (a street off Prince Edward Rd. West), Kowloon. MTR: Prince Edward (then follow the signs). Open all day.

You'll find an overwhelming amount of flowers and tropical plants here. The star of the show – and the unofficial flower of Hong Kong – are tropical orchids and lilies, and here you'll find a plethora of varieties of both. Amid the slew of wholesalers and retailers (most are happy to engage in either type of sales), you might consider an oriental plant pot or vase as a souvenir; or bring home some flower, vegetable or herb seeds.

Goldfish Market

North section of Tung Choi St., Mong Kok, Kowloon. MTR: Mong Kok (coming back from the Prince Edward MTR station, cross two parallel streets, Fa Yuen St. and Tung Choi St.). Open all day.

After birds, fish are the second most popular pet of the Chinese, who attribute a multitude of feng shui virtues to them. Traditionally, the Chinese will buy 3, 6 or 8 fish, all lucky numbers. Gold-colored fish are said to bring fortune; the black ones protect one's dwelling. As you walk through this market, note the incredible variety of fish in the store window aquariums.

Ladies' Market

South section of Tung Choi St., Kowloon. MTR: Mong Kok. Open year-round daily from 5pm until late at night.

Following Tung Choi Street to the south beyond Argyle Street, you enter another market, one that's not just for ladies, despite its name. Clothing sold here is primarily for women, but clothes for men and children are available too – not to mention sunglasses, watches and fake designer handbags.

STREET MARKETS

125

LOCAL CRAFTS

There is little that is made by hand in Hong Kong today. Rare exceptions include a handful of paper makers around Staunton Street in SoHo – where once many of these artisans held sway alongside print workshops before these spaces were converted into chic restaurants, bars and boutiques. Personalized seals to stamp on letters and documents are still hand-carved, as are some jade and a few other semi-precious gems. However, most of the stones are now carved in Mainland China or Southeast Asia where labor costs are lower.

Calligraphy

Long practiced as an art form in China, calligraphy is indeed "beautiful writing" and something to be revered.

Skilled calligraphers often play with the speed and pressure of their strokes in order to convey the emotions in a particular text. While in the West, it may be hard to imagine many people wanting to frame a hand-painted English-language poem or a saying, when it is painstakingly scribed with ink and brush in Chinese, such a thing is dearly treasured. If you want an original gift, look for talented practitioners of the calligraphic arts in the stalls at the **Temple Street Night Market★★★** (see Street Markets) and at seasonal festivals.

Carved Seals

Seals (ink stamps) carved out of stone or bone are one of the four treasures of the traditional Chinese literary tool set (paper, ink, inkstone and brush). Many seal engravers set up in "**Chop Alley**," as **Man Wa Lane** is known, in one of the most Chinese quarters of the city (Sheung Wan, Hong Kong Island. MTR: Sheung Wan). Allow 24 hours for the craftsmen to engrave a polished stone seal with your name on it in Chinese characters or Roman letters (prices average around HK$100).

Jade

China's most precious gem, jade (or Yu) is composed of several minerals. The most expensive, opaque green jadeite from

Carved seals for sale in "Chop Alley"

© Alex Havret/Apa Publications

How To Choose Jade

A semi-precious stone, jade is available in every possible shade of green, from the deepesr emerald to the palest sage. The generic term "jade" covers two different minerals, jadeite and nephrite, and the two are very difficult to tell apart. Generally speaking, the green tinges found in a piece of natural jade should stand up to the light test: hold the jade up to a light source; if it reveals a uniform color, it's actually a piece of colored glass. Another, and more dangerous, test is to fire your stone in the flame of a blowtorch; if it is nephrite, the flame will turn yellow. It is often difficult to be sure of the authenticity of jade jewelry, so be sure to purchase it from a reputable dealer. Real jade will last a lifetime, and the more you wear it, the more brilliant and translucent the stone will become. If you look closely, you will see that the nuances of green change over time too.

Xinjiang is very rare. With its nuances of green and duller appearance, nephrite takes on tones of yellow, white or black. The first jades, discovered on the site of Hemadu, date from 5000 BC. Because jade is said to have the power to prolong life, it was used in funeral rites. It only became an art object in the 18C.

Today you'll see jade carved into a range of shapes including vases and likenesses of people, birds, animals, flowers and dragons. For the best selection in Hong Kong, check out the **Jade Market★** in Kowloon *(Kansu and Shanghai Sts., Yau Ma Tei; open daily 10am–3:30pm; see Street Markets)*.

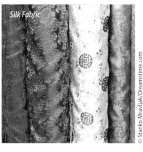

Silk Fabric

© Stanko Mravljak/Dreamstime.com

or jackets with vibrant hand-stitched images – can be found at area markets and Chinese department stores *(see Shopping)*. Silk items are quite affordable here, compared to European prices.

Silk

This most noble of fabrics was first made in China and was the source of the Middle Kingdom's fortune at one time. Traced back to the Shang Dynasty (c.1600–1100 BC), the making of silk is predominant in Shanghai, Nankin and Suzhou; brocade is a specialty of the Chengdu region in Sichuan. Though not made in Hong Kong, fine Chinese embroidered silk clothing – such as dressing gowns

Touring Tip

In China, bartering is the rule, except at supermarkets and in state-run stores. Bartering is well received by most all vendors, as long as it is accompanied with a smile and patience. Avoid haggling, however, over a few *yuans* with farmers. Don't hesitate to negotiate two-thirds or even three-fourths of the displayed price of an item (except for certain goods such as electronics).

LOCAL CRAFTS

NIGHTLIFE

For the visitor, the after-dark action is most accessible on the north shore of Hong Kong Island between Central and Wan Chai, and in Tsim Sha Tsui in Kowloon. The bars of Hong Kong Island are where you'll find most of the resident Westerners. Happy hour in Central's **Lan Kwai Fong** is packed with office workers who come by for an after-work libation, with the merriment often spilling out into the street. The district's bars are relatively expensive and stay open into the wee morning hours (usually around 2am). Near Lan Kwai Fong, SoHo (South of Hollywood Road, the area around the lower part of the Mid-Levels Escalator) fans out parallel to Staunton and Elgin streets, where you'll find more affordable watering holes that tend to close earlier than those in Lan Kwai Fong.

Wan Chai also wakes up at night, and a large number of fashionable venues have opened their doors here. (There are only a few of the old strip clubs left, owing to redevelopment over the past couple of decades.) Ditto for Causeway Bay, behind Times Square on **Yiu Wah Street**, where the stylish Hong Kongese party set congregates. In Tsim Sha Tsui, bars nestle together around ☕ **Knutsford Terrace** and the Knutsford Steps. In all these areas, however, you can find some fine freestanding bars in buildings off the main drag, as well as in hotels.

BARS

Aqua Spirit

1 Peking Rd., 29th floor, Tsim Sha Tsui, Kowloon. MTR: Tsim Sha Tsui. 3427 2288. www.aqua.com.hk.

Stylish and theatrical, Aqua Spirit affords a sweeping view of the harbor and Hong Kong Island. This popular spot teems with upper-crust locals and tourists for a good reason: Aqua Spirit's well-crafted signature cocktails.

Café Gray Bar

49th floor, The Upper House, Pacific Place, 88 Queensway, Admiralty., Hong Kong Island. MTR: Admiralty. 2918 1838. www.upperhouse.com.

This candlelit bar boasts super views of the skyscrapers of Hong Hong Island and across Victoria Harbour to Kowloon.

Knutsford Terrace Nightlife

Hong Kong Tourism Board

A refined menu of bar snacks, and an exceptionally friendly and knowledgeable bar staff enhance the experience.

Club 71

67 Hollywood Rd., Central (entrance through a little alleyway at 69 Hollywood Rd.). MTR: Central. 2858 7071.

Taking its name from July 1, 2003 – the date of the territory's

MUST DO

Yum Cha!

Too much partying on Saturday night? Perhaps you can soothe that hangover by indulging in a favorite Chinese tradition on Sunday: *yum cha*. Literally meaning "to have tea," *yum cha* denotes a family gathering for dim sum – either at home or at a local restaurant. If you choose the latter, once your group is seated, you will choose your tea from a selection of jasmine, oolong or pu'er. During the meal, you'll barely empty your teapot before it is filled again. Then you order your food, which is wheeled to the table on rolling carts. Dim sum is available in myriad versions of small buns, dumplings and other small dishes, which are constantly updated by the chefs.

first large-scale pro-democratic demonstrations in Hong Kong (still held annually) – this bar is one of SoHo's little-known treasures. Its peaceful terrace and vibrant decor attract artists, intellectuals and dreamers.

Felix

The Peninsula Hong Kong, Salisbury Rd., Tsim Sha Tsui, Kowloon. MTR: Tsim Sha Tsui. 2920 2888. www.peninsula.com.

Designer Philippe Starck made his mark at this ultramodern lounge on the 28th floor of The Peninsula, which offers breathtaking views over the Hong Kong landscape. Cocktails are superb, and of the three bars, the Long Table boasts the best cityscape. Much was made of the vertiginous view of Kowloon experienced by gentlemen visiting the urinals; it is impressive, but is no longer a unique experience.

 Oyster Bar & Grill

Sheraton Hong Kong Hotel & Towers, 18th floor, 20 Nathan Rd., Tsim Sha Tsui, Kowloon. MTR: Tsim Sha Tsui. 2369 1111, ext 3145. www.starwoodhotels.com.

Understated elegance here allows the view to shine – and what a

view! If you're in the mood for a splurge, select from the menu of fresh oysters, displayed on ice at the counter and shucked to order.

The Pawn

62 Johnston Rd., Wan Chai. MTR: Wan Chai., Hong Kong Island. 2866 3444.

With a pub on the first floor and a restaurant on the second, this former pawnbroker's shop attracts a trendy crowd. Choose from cocktails, beers on tap and a fine selection of whiskey. Pub customers have access to the upstairs balcony, but the rooftop terrace caters to private parties.

Peak Café

9-13 Shelly St., Central. MTR: Central. 2140 6877. cafedecogroup.com.

Easy on the eye with its Art Deco atmosphere, this bar/restaurant has an excellent cocktail list as well as a fine Western menu. The café's long open front makes a perfect perch for watching SoHo make merry.

NIGHTLIFE

Sense 99

99F Wellington St., 2nd floor,
Central. **MTR: Central.**
www.sense99.com.

Stop at the front door, buzz the intercom and climb the narrow staircase to enter this bilevel bar run by a group of friends. On the first floor, you'll find the bar and a handful of tables; upstairs is a space for improv performances – music and comedy – and a balcony where you can sit outside and bathe in the bright neon lights of Central.

Sevva

Prince's Building, 25th floor,
10 Chater Rd., Central. **MTR: Central**
2537 1388. www.sevva.hk.

With its outstanding wraparound wooden deck, and its cluster of comfy sofas and tall tables inside, this cocktail bar is part of a restaurant that is owned by a prominent socialite.
The cocktails and atmosphere are both great; the latter features good tunes on the sound system, and occasionally, live performers.

Staunton's

10-12 Stauntons St., Central.
MTR: Central. *2973 6611.*
www.stauntonsgroup.com.

A cross between a wine bar, a pub and a café, this well-established SoHo hangout also serves snacks, salads and hamburgers in case you're feeling peckish at midnight.

LIVE MUSIC

The Fringe Club

2 Lower Albert Rd., Central.
MTR: Central. *2521 7251.*
www.hkfringe.com.hk.
See Performing Arts.

An arts center run by an NGO which promotes non-mainstream Hong Kong culture, the Fringe Club includes a ground-level bar where regular performances take place on a small tiny stage (often local groups differing in style from the habitual "Canto-pop"). There's also a bar on the rooftop terrace that proves to be quite popular when the weather is fair. On the last Saturday of every month, the Fringe Club organizes jazz concerts by local musicians.

The Fringe Club

Florent Bonnefoy/Michelin

Long Live the Pub

British rule may be gone, but the public house (pub) legacy survives on Hong Kong Island. A longtime favorite, **Dickens Bar** in the basement of the Excelsior Hotel (*2837 6782; www.madarinoriental.com*) in Causeway Bay, screens major soccer, rugby and cricket games and dishes up decent food. In SoHo, **The Globe** (*45-53 Graham St., Central; MTR: Central; 2543 1941; www.theglobe.com.hk*) was once an independent bar. Now relocated and re-invented as a gastro-pub, it serves modern pub fare and a large selection of international beers. The Globe also offers some interesting micro-brews, one or two of them from Hong Kong.

Ned Kelly's Last Stand

11a Ashley Rd., Tsim Sha Tsui, Kowloon. MTR: Tsim Sha Tsui. 2376 0562.

This laid-back pub, named after a once-notorious Australian bandit, is a good place for a beer. It has an acceptable pub menu too, but it's the Dixieland jazz band that keeps 'em coming back to Ned Kelly's. The band plays nightly starting at around 9pm, and the scene at Ned's gets particularly lively on weekend nights.

NIGHTCLUBS

Dragon-i

60 Wyndham St., The Centrium, Central. MTR: Central. 3110 1222. www.dragon-i.com.hk.

Anyone who is anyone in Hong Kong knows that Dragon-i is *the* place to see and be seen. David Beckham, Hugh Grant and a virtual constellation of other international stars have been known to drop by when they're in town. Done in designer Chinese décor with private rooms and an outdoor terrace, the venue morphs into a cool restaurant offering Cantonese dim sum and Japanese fare during the day.

Drop

On Luk Mansion, 39-43 Hollywood Rd., Central. MTR: Central. 2543 8856, www.drophk.com.

Known for its fresh fruit-infused martinis, its beautiful crowd and its rockin' DJs, this basement club ranks as one of the city's hottest spots to drink and boogie. You might even catch risqué performing acts, such as pole-dancing.

Yumla

79 Wyndham St., ground floor of Harilela House, Central (go down stepped pedestrian-only Pottinger St. from the police station on Hollywood Rd.). MTR: Central. 2147 2383. www.yumla.com.

Yumla looks more like a bar than a nightclub, but in any case it's the hip place for electronic music fans in Hong Kong. The small space often fills to bursting, and it's not unusual for the party to overflow onto the stairs of the neighboring garden. A warm atmosphere is guaranteed.

SPAS

In Hong Kong, most luxury hotels would feel incomplete without a spa, and some fine freestanding day spas have also debuted here recently. In a reflection of the destination itself, many of the therapies offered incorporate both Eastern and Western elements.

Chuan Spa at Langham Place

Langham Place, 555 Shanghai St., Mong Kok, Kowloon. **MTR: Mong Kok.** *3552 3510. www.chuan spa.com.*

Ever-evolving treatments in this dark wood and slate ambience combine well-executed Eastern and Western techniques. For a real tension reliever, treat yourself to the Tao of Detox – a 2.5-hour package featuring a de-stressing scrub, a massage and a facial that claims to have uplifting results.

Elemis Day Spa

Century Square, 1 D'Aguilar St., 9th floor, Central, Hong Kong Island. **MTR: Central.** *2521 6660. www.elemisdayspa.com.hk.*

Both executives and stay-at-home moms come to de-stress with the spa rituals at this urban oasis, which caters its treatments to both men and women. The oh-so-soothing Elemis Modern Skin Facial continues its deeply hydrating effects for up to a day after it is applied.

Gentlemen's Tonic

The Landmark, B47–B48, Basement 1 Level, Central. **MTR: Central.** *2525 2455. www.gentlemenstonic.com.*

Finally, a place just for men. This London-born gents' spa opened a Hong Kong outpost in June 2011. In addition to massages, Tonic offers a barbershop as well as salon services (facials, hair removal, manicures and pedicures).

Oriental Spa

Landmark Mandarin Oriental, 15 Queen's Rd., Central. **MTR: Central.** *2132 0011. www.mandarinoriental.com.*

The Other TCM: Traditional Chinese Massage

Hong Kong's best spas are all about pampering – you indicate how much pressure will be applied, and sometimes you even choose the aromatherapy oil best suited to you that day. Not all traditional Chinese massage forms are quite that gentle, but their effects are legendary. Traditional Chinese massage and reflexology (applying pressure to specific points on the feet or hands) target pressure points and meridian lines along the body.

These points are believed to release tension or, in the case of reflexology, are thought to correspond to and target other areas or internal organs in the body. Manipulations are usually quite strong and are applied without oil and through clothing (a loose top and shorts or long pants are often provided for guests to wear).

Oriental Spa

Mandarin Oriental Hotel Group

Gracious therapists focus entirely on you at this cozy boutique spa of the highest order. The Oriental Spa's Time Ritual is a personalized combination of body and face treatments determined by an initial consultation with a therapist. Facilities include studios for both Pilates and Ashtanga Yoga.

The Plateau

Grand Hyatt Hong Kong, 1 Harbour Rd., Wan Chai, Hong Kong Island. MTR: Wan Chai. 2588 2802. www.hyatt.com.

Treatments here run the gamut from a salt and pepper body scrub to a Shiatsu massage, while cool marble rooms, water features, and spacious changing areas give you a true sense of escape and pampering at this award-winning spa. Therapists here are top-notch, and they discreetly check in on you without invading your privacy.

Ritz-Carlton Spa by ESPA

International Commerce Centre, 1 Austin Rd. West, Kowloon. MTR: Kowloon. 3717 2040. www.ritzcarlton.com.

Top UK spa operator ESPA fashioned this large contemporary space in chocolate brown wood and subtle lighting. Signature treatments use some Chinese strokes for tension release; a good one to try is the two-hour Advanced Back, Face and Scalp Treatment with hot stones.

Sense of Touch

52 D'Aguilar St., 1st–5th floor, Central. MTR: Central. 2526 6918. www.senseoftouch.com.hk.

A well-designed respite from the moment you walk into its dim denlike setting from the bustling streets of Hong Kong Island, Sense of Touch customizes many of its wellness treatments for both genders. The Cheers to Beers package is a must-do for men; it features a calming soak in a dark ale bath, followed by a barley scrub and a deep-tissue massage.

Spa at The Four Seasons Hong Kong

8 Finance St., 6th floor, Central. MTR: Central. 3196 8900. www.fourseasons.com.

Spacious, minimalist and warm, this spa boasts saunas in its changing rooms as well as a "vitality pool" filled with warm high-mineral-content water. Touch separate buttons to activate the massage jets and/or a small waterfall to massage your head and shoulders. From a long list of treatments – many with hybrid components – the Four Seasons Fusion Massage is a winner, combining Chinese acupressure, Hawaiian lomi lomi, Swedish massage and stretching.

SPAS

133

RESTAURANTS

Hong Kong's international reputation as a foodie paradise is well deserved. The Hong Kongese, like all Chinese, have a real passion for table and service arts. As the Chinese believe, you must live to eat, but if you do it well, you will live better and for a longer time.

$ less than HK$80
$$ HK$80-150
$$$ HK$150-300
$$$$ over HK$300

Price and Amenities

The restaurants below were selected for their ambience, location, variety of regional dishes and/or value for money. Prices indicate the average cost of an appetizer, main course, and dessert for one person, not including beverages, taxes or gratuities. Most restaurants are open daily (except where noted), and most, but not all, accept major credit cards.

Cuisine

In Hong Kong, you'll find authentic dishes from all other regions of China, as well as Southeast Asia, but Cantonese menus are the most abundant. Cantonese cuisine aims to bring out the true taste of ingredients by steaming or sautéeing them in a wok; if a sauce is added, it is there to enhance the flavor of the food, not to mask it. Given that Hong Kong is surrounded by water, it's no surprise that fish and shellfish are widely available. And although Western restaurants have long been a part of Hong Kong's culinary scene, this fare tends to be more expensive, since many of the ingredients are flown in from afar. The Chinese diet traditionally uses a combination of *yin* ("cold") and *yang* ("hot") foods in order to maintain balance in the body. Raw and cooked, hot and cold, crunchy and soft, dry and sticky, sour, sweet, and bitter —these tastes are all combined to reinforce one's vital energy, or *qi*.

Local Flavor

Be sure to try at least one of the simple restaurants called *cha chaan teng*, literally meaning "tea diner." A Hong Kong invention, tea diners mix Eastern and Western café food. French toast with milk tea is as popular as fried noodles in these places. **Milk tea** is an adaptation of what British colonists drank years ago; but in this version, the tea is brewed longer, lightened with canned evaporated milk and sweetened to taste with sugar. For traditional Cantonese fare, eating **dim sum** is essential. For the uninitiated, dim sum is a meal of small dishes, made for sharing – eaten any time from breakfast to mid-afternoon. Most often it comprises steamed or fried dumplings, whose wheat- or rice-

Dim Sum

Lacquered meats on restaurant windows

© Amanda Hall/age fotostock

flour skin is filled with chopped combinations of seasoned meat, seafood and vegetables. Another specialty, **lacquered meats** can be seen shimmering in restaurant windows. They are generally called *siu mei*, which indicates the cooking method (meat is roasted on a spit above a fire).

Among the more suprising dishes are the famed **hundred-year-old eggs** – duck eggs preserved for several weeks in a mix of hay and lime. Translucent and greenish in appearance, the eggs may not look appetizing, but they are truly delicious.

A Taste of Macau

Culinary snack specialties in the former Portuguese colony of Macau include tasty strips of dried meat. The meat, usually pork, is marinated in honey, then seasoned, grilled, dried and cut into rectangles. In tourist areas, vendors of this snack will entice you with sample tastes. **Heong Kei** (*6 Travessa do Auto Novo; 2893 8400*), serves some fine examples. Macau's best-known sweet treat is its **Portuguese egg tarts**.

Crumblier than the Cantonese version, the pastry is filled with rich custard, the top of which is caramelized and slightly burnt (similar to a crème brulée). **Lord Stowe's Bakery** (*see p 90*) makes some of the best egg tarts on the island, despite the fact that the founder is an Englishman.

The Food Scene Today

A few years ago, the SoHo neighborhood in Central on Hong Kong Island was alone in offering intimate restaurants, with menus from around the globe. Now, you can find such spots in pockets of Wan Chai, Causeway Bay and Sheung Wan, while Tsim Sha Tsui in Kowloon has added bars and restaurants around its lively Knutsford Terrace area.

More recently, a renovation of Harbour City, next to the Star Ferry terminal, welcomed new open-fronted establishments with great water views.

Upscale hotels offer some of the finest Western and Chinese fare in Hong Kong, their restaurants affiliated with celebrity chefs like Nobu Matsuhisa, Pierre Gagnière and Alain Ducasse.

Hong Kong Island

Brunch Club
$ **European**
70 Peel St., Central. **MTR: Central.**
2526 8861. www.brunch-club.org.
You'll enjoy the cozy atmosphere
of this place that specializes in –
you guessed it – brunch, at any
time of the day. Grilled cheese,
salads and more are here, for
mornings when you can't face
sautéed noodles.

🍴 Mak's Noodle
$ **Cantonese**
77 Wellington St., Central.
MTR: Central. *2544 4556.*

Mak's Noodle
Michelin

Famed for their noodles, this
family-owned and operated
restaurant (the grandfather was
crowned "won ton king" in the
1930s) has served the likes of
Travel Channel chef Anthony
Bourdain. And for good reason:
bowls of springy egg noodles
and stuffed won tons come in a
fragrant broth flavored with dried
fish, shrimp and pork bones.

🍴 Ngau Kee Food Café
$ **Cantonese**
3 Gough St., Central.
MTR: Central. *2546 2584.*
A good old Cantonese tea diner

(*cha chaan teng*), Ngau Kee offers
reasonable prices, simple but
tasty dishes, and curt service. Try
the braised stuffed eggplant, and
the ginger chicken, Chiuchow-
style, based on a recipe from the
Guangdong province of China.

🍴 Super Star Seafood Restaurant
$ **Cantonese**
*Times Square, 10th floor, Causeway
Bay.* **MTR: Causeway Bay.** *2628
0886. www.superstarrest.com.hk.*
Super Star's main attraction is its
dim sum. (Folks certainly don't
come here for the décor, which
includes plastic ivy and pink
flowers.) Crispy roast pork, *char
siu* (barbecued pork) buns, shrimp
dumplings and *cheung fan* (rice
flour rolls) never fail to win raves.

Tsim Chai Kee
$ **Cantonese**
98-102 Wellington St.
MTR: Central. *2850 6471.*
This restaurant, one of the least
expensive in Central, is extremely
popular. You won't have many
options, as the only fare on offer
is delicious noodles with toppings
of shrimp-stuffed won tons, fish or
beef. There's a second location at
61 Connaught Road.

Lin Heung Teahouse
$$ **Cantonese**
*160-164 Wellington St., Sheung
Wan.* **MTR: Sheung Wan.**
2544 4556.
Even the most naturalized
foreigners feel out of their element
here. Hong Kongese of every
walk of life share big tables to
enjoy dim sum like you won't
find anywhere else. Don't expect
special treatment from the wait

MUST EAT

Lin Heung Teahouse

Florent Bonnefoy/Michelin

staff, but do point out the baskets that tempt you as the carts roll by. If your food is taking too long to arrive, make your way to the kitchen exit to be the first served.

 Mist

$$ **Japanese**
4 Sun Wai Rd., Causeway Bay.
MTR: Causeway Bay. 2881 5006.
www.mist.com.hk.
This elegant Japanese ramen noodle bar is a franchise of Chef Yasuji Morizumi's award-winning Japanese brand, which brings French flair to a Japanese staple. Soup noodles here are made from natural ingredients and high-grade flour, resulting in a fresh soft noodle with some bite. Of the five soups available, the soy is an elegant take on a Tokyo favorite, while *karamiso* kicks up a miso blend. All are topped with melt-in-your-mouth slices of barbecued pork. Mist also has a handful of tasty non-noodle dishes.

Tak Kee Chiu Chow Restaurant
$$ **Chiuchow**
535 Queen's Rd. West, Sheung Wan.
MTR: Sheung Wan. 2819 5568.
Chiuchow cuisine is one of the most delicious in all of China, and this restaurant has a good reputation around Hong Kong. Feast on crispy sausage with sticky rice, oyster pancakes, congee (rice porridge) with meat, poached bean leaves, and Chiuchow sweet and sour noodles. If that's not adventurous enough, try the salted lemon Sprite.

Thai Delight
$$ **Thai**
117 Lockhart Rd., Wan Chai.
MTR: Wan Chai. 2877 7983.
www.thaidelight.com.hk.
Located in one of the sleazier streets of Wan Chai, this restaurant offers well-prepared Thai food. All-you-can-eat menus are available on weekends and holidays (11:30am–3:30pm) for HK$138, and set lunches cost half that price.

Tonkichi Tonkatsu Seafood
$$ **Japanese**
World Trade Centre, 280 Gloucester Rd., Causeway Bay. 2577 6617.
Specializing in *tonkatsu* (a breaded and deep-fried Japanese-style pork cutlet) this restaurant never seems to slow down. You'll have to stand in line to taste their tender and light breaded pork scallops and vegetables – variations on the traditional theme.

 Café Deco
$$$ **International**
1-2/F, Peak Galleria, 118 Peak Rd., Victoria Peak. Accessible via the Peak Tram. 2849 5111.
www.cafedecogroup.com.
Art Deco accents punctuate this lofty two-level dining room, where a window table is de rigueur. Featuring fresh seafood, pastas, salads, burgers, pizza and curries, the international menu leans heavily toward Western fare. It's a great spot for Sunday brunch.

RESTAURANTS

Luk Yu Tea House

$$$ Cantonese
24 Stanley Rd., Central.
MTR: Central. 2523 5464.
A prominent feature in Hong Kong's dim sum scene, this esteemed establishment – one of the last teahouses in the area – serves its clients in a setting lined with wood, cozy booths and whirring fans overhead. Clad in white shirts, the waiters are known for their brusqueness – unless you are a regular. It's worth putting up with a bit of attitude for the outstanding dim sum.

Tsui Hang Village

$$$ Cantonese
New World Tower, 2nd floor, 16-18 Queen's Rd., Central.
MTR: Central. 2524 2012.
The flagship of a small respected group of Cantonese restaurants has been renovated in cool gray tones. You can dine like an emperor on many a classic here. Barbecued meats are spot-on, but for a real treat, try the chicken with preserved vegetables, shredded pork and mushrooms, baked in a lotus leaf (this dish must be ordered in advance).

Yung Kee

$$$ Cantonese
32-40 Wellington St., Central.
MTR: Central. 2522 1624.
www.yungkee.com.hk.
Favored by locals – as much for its noisy, colorful atmosphere as for its authentic Cantonese cooking – Yung Kee serves up some of the best grilled lacquered goose and pork around. Dim sum is served from 2pm to 5pm. Reservations are a good idea.

Lacquered goose, Yung Kee

Yung Kee

Zen

$$$ Cantonese
Pacific Place, 88 Queensway, Admiralty. **MTR: Admiralty.** *2845 4555. www.pacificplace.com.hk.*
At Zen, the décor may be contemporary but the cooking is traditional Cantonese fare done right. Small portions of house signatures make it easy to try multiple dishes, and the steamed rice-flour rolls here have a larger variety of fillings than on most dim sum menus. The adventurous end their meal with the steamed papaya, filled with dried snow frog and coconut milk; it is said to be good for the complexion.

Amber

$$$$ French
Landmark Mandarin Oriental, 15 Queen's Rd., Central. **MTR: Central.** *2132 0188. www.mandarin oriental.com/landmark.*
This elegant contemporary dining room packs its tables at lunchtime with executive types snapping up the prix-fixe meals. Dutch-born Executive Chef Richard Ekkubus has been on a creative roll since Amber launched in 2005, using top-tier ingredients in his refined French cuisine. Reservations are recommended.

MUST EAT

Fook Lam Moon

$$$$ **Cantonese**

35-45 Johnston Rd., Wan Chai.
MTR: Wan Chai. 2866 0663.

A favorite among Hong Kong's high-rollers, Fook Lam Moon serves some of the most expensive dishes around – abalone, shark's fin and sea cucumbers – and prepares them using premium ingredients.

Gaia Ristorante

$$$$ **Italian**

Grand Millennium Plaza,
181 Queen's Rd., Sheung Wan.
MTR: Sheung Wan. 2167 8200.
www.gaiagroup.com.hk.

A pleasant outdoor terrace and fresh food, including pasta dishes that win the hearts of members of the local Italian community, all adds up to a top restaurant. At lunch, locals love the daily antipasto buffet, which is easily a meal in itself. At dinner, pasta dishes vie with the likes of grilled milk-fed veal loin for your attention.

Gold

$$$$ **Italian**

LKF Tower, 2nd floor, 33 Wyndham St., Central. MTR: Central. 2869 9986. www.gold-dining.com. Closed Sun.

Chef/owner Harlan Goldstein, a.k.a. "chef to Hong Kong's tycoons" recently opened this contemporary Italian restaurant. The dining room is simply decorated and has a small terrace. If you go, don't miss the exceptional handmade pappardelle pasta with wild mushrooms, truffles and smoked egg. A serious wine cellar includes a few reasonably priced offerings both by the bottle and the glass.

Liberty Exchange

$$$$ **American**

Two Exchange Square, ground floor, 8 Connaught Pl., Central. MTR: Central. 2810 8400. www.lex.hk.

In this bi-level restaurant, the downstairs has a bistro vibe with an open front, while the upper level is more formal. Fish plays a key role on the menu, but the signature Statue burger, served with basil mayonnaise and crispy fries, nods to both America and the restaurant's name. The bar is popular with bankers who work in the building.

Lung King Heen

$$$$ **Cantonese**

Four Seasons Hotel Hong Kong, 8 Financial St., Central. MTR: Central. 3196 8888. www.four seasons.com/hongkong.

Perched on the fourth floor of the Four Seasons hotel, Lung King Heen (or "View of the Dragon" in Cantonese) is probably the most sumptuous Cantonese restaurant in Hong Kong. Here, you'll experience refined cuisine with innovative twists and excellent service. The large picture windows offer a stunning view over Victoria Harbour.

Lung King Heen

Four Seasons Hotel Hong Kong

Island Shangri-La Hotel

Petrus

One Harbour Road

$$$$ Cantonese
Grand Hyatt Hotel, 1 Harbour Rd.,
Wan Chai. MTR: Wan Chai. 2588
1234, ext 7338. www.hyatt.com.
This expansive split-level Art
Deco dining room serves A-list
Cantonese cuisine. One of its most-
ordered dishes is its Beijing duck,
roasted, then carved tableside.
Roll the slices in pancakes with
plum sauce and sliced vegetable
condiments yourself or ask the
waiter to prepare them for you.
Barbecued meats here are a cut
above many kitchens, and the
service is particularly friendly and
courteous.

Opus Grill

$$$$ Steakhouse
LKF Tower, 7th floor, 33 Wyndham
St., Central. MTR: Central. 2526
2366. www.opusgrill.com.
In this popular grill room, with its
sizeable bar, you'll find great food
at a premium price.
Though the focus is on hormone-
free, farm-raised steaks from the
US and Australia, Opus is not just
all about red meat. The menu also
cites roast chicken and grilled
seafood, including Atlantic salmon
served with barbecue sauce,
salmon roe coleslaw and spicy
potato salad.

Petrus

$$$$ French
Island Shangri-La Hotel, Pacific
Place, 88 Queensway, Admiralty.
MTR: Admiralty. 2820 8590.
www.shangri-la.com.
Crystal chandeliers and a
breathtaking harbor view from
the 56th floor set the scene for a
memorable meal here. Regarded
as one of the top fine-dining
restaurants in town, Petrus
changes its menu frequently
to take advantage of seasonal
products. Knowledgeable service
and more than 20,000 bottles of
old and new world wines add to
the gourmet experience. Jackets
are required for gentlemen.

The Press Room

$$$$ French
108 Hollywood Rd., Central.
MTR: Central. 2525 3444.
www.thepressroom.com.hk.
Closely packed tables at this casual
brasserie are usually full. The
reason: no-nonsense French fare
made from top-quality ingredients
and served without pretension.
Le vin is a big draw here, with some
uncommon producers represented
on the wine list.

Totts & Roof Terrace

$$$$ Contemporary
Excelsior Hotel, 281 Gloucester Rd.,
Causeway Bay. MTR: Causeway
Bay. 2837 6786. www.mandarin
oriental.com/excelsior.
For alfresco dining, you can't beat
the rooftop terrace on the 34th
floor of the Excelsior. The fabulous
view is rivaled only by dishes such
as a contemporary take on *pot au
feu* made with Spanish lamb, and
an assiette of duck with parsnip
purée and cherry jus.

MUST EAT

Kowloon

Domon Sapporo Ramen

$ **Japanese**

22A Grand Building, Granville Circuit (off Granville Rd., behind Park Hotel and the Kowloon Ramada Inn), Tsim Sha Tsui. **MTR: Tsim Sha Tsui. 2739 9431.**

This small noodle restaurant is similar to those found in Japan, where you can see the cooks hard at work behind the counter. The *ramen* are delicious, as are the pot-sticker dumplings. It's no frills in terms of décor and service.

Khyber Pass

$ **Indo-Pakistani**

Chungking Mansions, Block E, 36-40 Nathan Rd., Tsim Sha Tsui. **MTR: Tsim Sha Tsui. 2739 1177.**

This inexpensive 7th-floor restaurant serves up some mighty good Indo-Pakistani dishes in the Chungking Mansions. The *vindaloo* will thrill spice lovers.

Gaylord's

$$ **Indian**

22-25 Ashley Rd., Tsim Sha Tsui. **MTR: Tsim Sha Tsui. 2736 1001. www.chiram.com.hk.**

With modest prices – especially the lunch buffet – an enthusiastic staff and appealing dishes that range from Goan fish curry to saag paneer, it's no wonder that this place has been going strong for nearly 40 years.

House of Jasmine

$$ **Cantonese**

Ocean Centre, Harbour City, Tsim Sha Tsui. **MTR: Tsim Sha Tsui. 2992 0232. www.maxims.com.hk.**

The outdoor terrace is the best place to sit in nice weather at this Cantonese restaurant in Harbour City. Enjoy a sea vista along with dim sum and Cantonese dishes prepared with a creative touch. You won't find any MSG in the signature crispy fried chicken, or in any of the dishes here.

Lei Garden

$$$ **Cantonese**

Houston Centre, 63 Mody Rd., Tsim Sha Tsui. **MTR: Tsim Sha Tsui. 2722 1636. www.leigarden.com.hk.**

This restaurant, with satellites in Singapore and Mainland China, delights seafood lovers and fans of traditional dim sum. Expect helpful service and a refined red and gold color scheme in the dining room to brighten your experience.

Gaddi's

$$$$ **French**

Peninsula Hotel, Salisbury Rd., Tsim Sha Tsui. **MTR: Tsim Sha Tsui. 2315 3171. Closed Sun.**

With its blue and gold carpet and luxurious appointments, Gaddi's offers dining fit for royalty; and only the best will do for both the wine and cuisine here. Reserve the chef's table in the kitchen for a close-up view of how the team pulls it all together. Jackets are required for gentlemen.

Gaddi's

© circa 2011 The Peninsula Hong Kong

🍴 Hutong

$$$$ **Northern Chinese**
1 Peking Rd., Tsim Sha Tsui.
***MTR: Tsim Sha Tsui.** 3428 8342,*
www.aqua.com.hk.

Taking its name from the Mandarin word for the small traditional courtyard streets of Beijing, Hutong sits on the 28th floor of the One Peking building, where antique Chinese wood screens and oversize bamboo bird cages are juxtaposed against views of the modern skyline. The likes of sweet and spicy glazed eel and Sichuan-style smoked duck with tea leaves will leave you wanting more.

Chilli prawns, Hutong

Aqua Group

Shang Palace

$$$$ **Cantonese**
Kowloon Shangri-La, 64 Mody Rd.,
Tsim Sha Tsui East. **MTR: Tsim Sha**
Tsui. *2733 8754. www.shangri-la.*
com/kowloon.

Four golden statues welcome you to this sumptuous room, with its red lacquer walls, where some of the best dim sum in Hong Kong is served. Entrées include some healthy dishes, such as sautéed rice topped with crab meat, egg white, wolfberries and diced mushrooms.

Macau

Traditional Cantonese fare in Macau is similar to that in Hong Kong, and well loved in the south of China. However, many visitors make a beeline for the restaurants serving Macanese food.

Born of the fusion between Portuguese and Chinese cooking, Macanese cuisine melds Mediterranean flavors with the exotic spices of southeastern Asia and Africa, also former Portuguese colonies.

$ less than MOP40
$$ MOP40-150
$$$ MOP150-300
$$$$ over MOP300

🍴 A Petisqueira

$$ **Portuguese**
15 Rua São João, Taipa Village.
2882 5354.

With checked tablecloths, a tile floor and faux grapes decorating the archways of the façade, this restaurant makes every effort to conjure up Portugal, right up to the flags hung on the walls. And as you would expect, the dishes (think paella, grilled cod and curried crab) are the real deal.

Leitaria I Son

$$ **Cantonese**
7 Largo do Senado, Peninsula
Macau. 2857 3638.

This little establishment enjoys a reputation that extends from Hong Kong to Canton, and beyond. The restaurant features milk-based desserts such as *seung pei lai* custard and milkshakes, but also makes excellent meat-filled steamed buns if you're hankering for something savory. Leitaria I Son has locations all over the city.

© Florent Bonnefoy/Michel n

🍴 A Lorcha

$$$ **Macanese**
*289 Rua do Almirante Sérgio,
Peninsula Macau. 2831 3193.
Closed Tue.*
Hidden behind a heavy
wooden door, A Lorcha mixes
up Portuguese and Macanese
cuisines. You'll adore their *pasteis
de bacalhau* (cod fritters) and *arroz
de marisco a portuguesa* (rice with
seafood). As for the Macanese
specialties, try the Portuguese-
style chicken served with a
coconut-curcuma sauce.

Restaurant Espaço Lisboa

$$$ **Portuguese**
*8 Rua das Gaivotas, Colôane
Village. 2888 2226.*
If you've come all the way to
Colôane, don't miss this tasty stop.
Take a seat on the balcony, where
tables are set up for admiring
the village rooftops. The simple
Portuguese cooking is a hit with
the locals. There's cod, of course,
but also Portuguese-style steak
and traditional vegetable soup.

Vida Rica

$$$ **Chinese**
*Mandarin Oriental Macau,
2nd floor, Avenida Dr Sun Yat Sen,
Nape District. 8805 8888.
www.mandarinoriental.com.*

Since it opened in 2010, Vida Rica
has been the "it" restaurant and bar
for the Macau elite.
Sea views and a stylish dark-wood
palette are the backdrop for a
restaurant that takes on both
Chinese and Western cuisine.
Dim sum is very popular here, as
are its premium cuts of grilled
meat, like grass-fed New Zealand
lamb and Black Angus beef
tenderloin.

Aux Beaux Arts

$$$$ **French**
*MGM Grand Hotel, Avenida Dr.
Sun Yat-Sen, Nape District. 8802
3888. www.mgmgrandmacau.
com.* A Belle Epoque vibe infuses
this Parisian-style brasserie at the
MGM Grand, whose authentic
French classics include *les cocottes*
– individual ceramic baking dishes
filled with savory stews such as
braised Dutch veal sweetbreads
with morels, bacon and potatoes.
Check out the Russian Room for
caviar and the Ice Bar for a glass
of bubbly.

🍴 Wing Lei

$$$$ **Cantonese**
*Wynn Macau, Rua Cidade de
Sintra, Nape District. 8986 3663.
www.wynnmacau.com.*
This relaxed contemporary take
on Cantonese fine dining does
have two imposing features: the
huge minimalist ceiling lanterns
that resemble illuminated artwork,
and a crystal dragon that twinkles
above the booth seating on one
wall. The menu presents exquisite
Cantonese cuisine, both in flavor
and presentation. Choose from
the set menu or à la carte items
such as braised sea cucumber and
barbecued suckling pig.

RESTAURANTS

143

HOTELS

Hong Kong boasts a wide range of accommodations for every budget and comfort level. The city's luxury high-end hotels are mostly spread between the Central, Admiralty, Wan Chai and Tsim Sha Tsui districts. All of those areas, plus Causeway Bay and North Point on Hong Kong Island and Mong Kok and Jordan in Kowloon, offer plenty of moderately priced hotels. Small guesthouses can be found on the Outlying Islands, while urban hostels range from spacious and comfortable places to no-frills crash pads. Macau hotels used to be mostly fairly simple, but with the transformation of Macau's casino scene, glitzy luxury accommodations are now plentiful on the island. The service standard in Hong Kong is excellent overall; well-trained hotel staff members are generally comfortable speaking English. Macau is still developing its world-class service – only the very high-end hotels can rival Hong Kong in this regard.

$ less than HK$340
$$ HK$340-500
$$$ HK$500-1000
$$$$ more than HK$1,000

Prices and Amenities

Accommodations described here are classified according to the price for a double room for one night, not including taxes or surcharges. Since these prices often vary considerably throughout the year, it is best to inquire beforehand and check the rates during the proposed period of your stay. Hotels accept major credit cards and all offer air-conditioning unless otherwise indicated. Many of the hotels listed in this guide also have first-class spas (see Spas) and restaurants (see Restaurants).

Online Booking

You'll often find better deals and promotions by booking online than if you book directly at the hotel (which will give you the higher published rack rate). Booking through travel agencies, or travel websites (at right) will also yield better prices. This holds true especially if you're staying more than one night. Normally, a 10-percent service charge will be added to any hotel rate.

The Hong Kong Tourism Board's website (www.discoverhong kong.com) has a feature called **Hotel Search**. Use it to choose from tens of thousands of rooms in dozens of hotels, with consistently monitored standards. Just select your pre-ferred location and amenities.

Alternatively, you can book hotel rooms while checking out the reviews from other travelers on the following websites:
www.asiarooms.com
www.asiatravel.com
www.wotif.com
www.hotels.com
www.expedia.com
www.ebookers.com

Hotels

Most standard hotels in Hong Kong belong to international or regional chains. This makes for a certain level of quality, and also a general comfort level – private bathrooms, televisions, telephones and air-conditioning are generally included – with more bells and whistles added in the higher price ranges. Varying tariffs are applied for extra beds or for more than two adult guests. During the off-season, discounts will systematically be applied to published rack rates.

Youth Hostels

www.yhachina.com/english/index. html (English-language online reservations).

Youth hostels do exist in Hong Kong and they are generally well maintained, employing staff that can speak good English. Double and single rooms are usually available in addition to dormitory beds. If you do not have a Hostelling International Card (you can buy one at the reception desk), you'll pay a little extra for your stay.

Hotel Reservations

Although English is spoken in most establishments (except for some budget properties), it is sometimes better to ask someone that speaks Cantonese to help you call for reservations.

High season corresponds with the three **"Golden Weeks"** (the vacation period) of Mainland China, when many visit Hong Kong: one week between mid-January and mid-February (for the Chinese New Year); the first week of May (Labor Day in China); and the first week of October (National Day holiday). Chinese tourists pack the attractions during these weeks, when hotel prices can more than double. At such times, it can be difficult to find a hotel room if you don't have a reservation. Summer is a peak period too,

as this is when many overseas guests visit the territory, so book in advance for July and August. September through November, the prime convention months, can be surprisingly busy too.

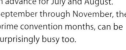

Hong Kong Island

Alisan Guest House
$$ **30 rooms**
Hoi To Court, 5th floor, Apt A, 275 Gloucester Rd. (entry on Cannon St.). Causeway Bay. 2838 0762. home.hkstar.com/~alisangh.
The helpfulness of owner Tommy Hou is one of the main selling points of this affordable guesthouse, conveniently located in Causeway Bay. The rooms may be small and modestly furnished, but they are clean and comfortable. The Alisan also offers 24-hour camera security.

Causeway Bay Guest House
$$ **7 rooms**
44 A-D Leighton Rd., Lai Yee Building, 1st floor, Apt B (enter through Leighton Lane and follow signs), Causeway Bay. 2895 2065. www.cbgh.net.
You're guaranteed a warm reception in this little guesthouse, where clean compact rooms come with a choice of one, two or three narrow beds. All rooms are equipped with air-conditioning and satellite TV, and a refrigerator and a microwave oven are available for guests' use.

Ibis North Point
$$ **75 rooms**
138 Java Rd., North Point. 2588 1111. www.accorhotels.com.
This large oceanfront building sits next to the North Point MTR

station. Here, you'll find simple business-oriented rooms just a stone's throw from Wan Chai and Causeway Bay. Request breakfast for a small additional charge.

Jockey Club Mt. Davis Youth Hostel
$$ 16 rooms
123 Mount Davis Path, Western District. 2817 5715. www.yhachina.com.
Probably the most accessible of all the youth hostels in the area, this property is located on Hong Kong Island at the top of Mount Davis. From this perch, it boasts a view over Victoria Harbour, along with double or quadruple rooms as well as dormitory beds.

Bishop Lei International House
$$$ 219 rooms
4 Robinson Rd., Mid-Levels. 2868 0828. www.bishopleihtl.com.hk.
Located in the heights of the Mid-Levels, this hotel may not give the warmest reception, but its best – and most expensive – rooms boast a good view of the port. No charge for Wi-Fi.

Newton Hotel
$$$ 362 rooms
218 Electric Rd., North Point. 2807 2333. www.newtonhk.com.
Slightly set back from the noisy heart of the island, the Newton features a friendly staff and rooms that are standard in décor. Executive-floor rooms make working a breeze, and amenities include a rooftop pool, sauna and gym. Ask for a room that faces the bay.

East
$$$$ 345 rooms
29 Taikoo Shing Rd., Taikoo Shing. 3968 3808. www.east-hongkong.com.
East caters to savvy business travelers with state-of-the-art communications technology: 37-inch, high-definition LCD TVs, iHome/iPods, and complimentary broadband and Wi-Fi Internet access throughout the hotel. A paperless front desk means you only have to check-in on your first visit; thereafter, you can use express check-in. For relaxation, try the outdoor heated pool.

The Excelsior
$$$$ 886 rooms
281 Gloucester Rd., Causeway Bay. 2894 8888. www.excelsiorhong kong.com.
The largest hotel on Hong Kong Island is run by the Mandarin Oriental group. Overlooking the Royal Hong Kong Yacht Club, it's a busy and pleasant place, with great restaurants and a good location in Causeway Bay. Rooms are compact and reasonably priced.

The Fleming
$$$$ 66 rooms
41 Fleming Rd., Wan Chai. 3607 2288. www.thefleming.com.hk.
With a charcoal gray façade and green-glass-enclosed balconies for its 66 spacious rooms, The Fleming is a hip hotel that suits creative types. Everything you need is here, from in-room high-speed Internet and small fully equipped kitchenettes to flat-screen TVs and goose-down duvets.

Four Seasons Hong Kong

$$$$ **399 rooms**
*8 Finance St., Central. 3196 8888.
www.fourseasons.com.*
Suitably grand in style and space,
this hotel claims some of the
best harbor views in Central –
particularly from the outdoor
pool deck, and the executive-club
lounge. Bright guestrooms are
some of the city's largest – not to
mention the 54 spacious suites.
Service is impeccable throughout.
At dinner, try the excellent
Cantonese cuisine at **Lung Keen
Hing** (*see Restaurants*).

 Grand Hyatt Hong Kong

$$$$ **549 rooms**
*1 Harbour Rd., Wan Chai. 2588
2802. www.hyatt.com.*
The Hyatt's lavish lobby, complete
with an indoor fountain, belies the
contemporary flair in the rooms.
A dramatic double staircase leads
up to the mezzanine Tiffin Lounge,
an elegant buffet restaurant with
live music. Other restaurants here
are longstanding local institutions.
You'll have harbor views from the
outdoor pool, and the three hotel
taxis are complementary for short
hops around the area.

Hotel LKF

$$$$ **95 rooms**
*33 Wyndham St., Lan Kwai Fong,
Central. 3518 9688. www.hotel-
LKF.com.hk.*
This property recently sprang up
in the hub of Hong Kong's nightlife
mecca, Lan Kwai Fong, from which
the hotel takes its name.
Spacious rooms are done in
masculine chocolate brown and
beige tones, and compact spaces
are enhanced by Bulgari amenities
and plenty of electronic gizmos,
including an in-room espresso
machine.

Island Shangri-La

$$$$ **531 rooms**
*Pacific Place, 88 Queensway,
Admiralty. 2877 3838.
www.shangri-la.com.*
Classic luxury begins here with
the staff in smart attire. In the
atrium, an expansive landscape,
Great Motherland of China, made
up of 250 Chinese silk panels, is
visible from some of the elevators.
For dinner, **The Lobster Bar &
Grill** comes highly rated.

Grand Hyatt Hong Kong

Hyatt Hotels

JIA Boutique Hotel

JIA Boutique Hotel

$$$$ 54 rooms

1-5 Irving St., Causeway Bay. 3196 9000. www.jiahongkong.com.
This boutique hotel, conceived with the help of French designer Philippe Starck and containing some of his furniture, presents rooms in the form of small apartments. In each of the three room categories (studio; one-bedroom suite; and a two-bedroom duplex penthouse), the space is clearly defined into living, dining and working areas, enhanced by a separate kitchenette and bathroom.

Landmark Mandarin Oriental

$$$$ 113 rooms

15 Queen's Rd., Central. 2132 0188. www.mandarin oriental.com.
A recent addition to Hong Kong's luxury properties, the Landmark was renovated in 2010. It features an open floor plan in the rooms, which are fitted with clean lines and a subtle color scheme. Expect a walk-in wardrobe, three flat-panel LCD televisions and an enhanced surround-sound system, plus an oversize round bathtub and rainforest shower in the bath.

Mandarin Oriental Hong Kong

$$$$ 502 rooms

5 Connaught Rd., Central. 2713 9211. www.mandarinoriental.com.
Established in 1963, this luxurious hotel is an icon in Hong Kong. All rooms were renovated in 2006 and are decorated with tasteful Chinese elements. Indulge yourself at the on-site spa, or just relax in your room and admire the port through the large picture windows.

Renaissance Harbour View Hotel

$$$$ 810 rooms

1 Harbour Rd., Wan Chai. 2802 8888. www.marriott.com.
The Renaissance enjoys a breathtaking view over Hong Kong, with the Hong Kong Exhibition Centre in the foreground. As with all Marriott Group properties, a large number of services are available, such as a sauna, salon, gym, and business center.

Rosedale on the Park

$$$$ 274 rooms

8 Shelter St., Causeway Bay. 2127 8888. www.rosedale.com.hk.
Rosedale's downtown location boasts open views of the harbor and Victoria Park. For even better cityscapes, check out the 33rd-

floor SkyZone Lounge. Rooms are small, but comfortable and well-equipped. A small gym and regular shuttle buses into Central round out the amenties.

Upper House
$$$$ **117 rooms**
Pacific Place, 88 Queensway, Admiralty. 2918 1838. www.upperhouse.com.
From a lobby that looks like a swish New York apartment building, elevators whisk guests up to stylish contemporary rooms that occupy the upper levels of this structure. A private garden and a library make unusual guest spaces, where you can have a drink or just relax. Besides fine food, **Café Gray Deluxe** has excellent city views.

Kowloon

Cosmic Guest House
$$ **79 rooms.**
54-64 Nathan Rd., Block A1, A2, F1 & F4, 12th floor, Mirador Mansions, Tsim Sha Tsui. 2369 6669. www.cosmicguesthouse.com.
One of the best lodgings in the Mirador Mansions, this guest house is run by friendly, young personnel. Rooms are all tiled and equipped with a small shower. Wi-Fi Internet access is complimentary, and dormitory beds are available for HK$80.

Dragon Hostel
$$ **36 rooms**
Sincere House, 7th floor, Apt 707, 83 Argyle St., Mong Kok. 2395 0577. www.dragonhostel.com.
In the heart of Mong Kok, this guest house prides itself on having welcomed visitors from all over the world for some twenty years now,

and it functions like a well-oiled machine. Internet and local calls are included in the room rate, and the staff will organize guided tours and visas. Don't forget to reserve, as the place is very popular.

Lee Garden House
$$ **37 rooms**
Block D, 8th floor, 34-36 Cameron Rd., Tsim Sha Tsui. 2367 2284. www.starguesthouse.com.hk.
Assets at Lee Garden House include rooms that are relatively large and well-equipped; and a staff that is happy to book guided tours and help with visa formalities. The owner has other guesthouses along the same lines of price and comfort (check the website for details).

Park Guest House
$$ **45 rooms.**
36-44 Nathan Rd., Block A1 (elevator 2) and F4, 15th floor, Chungking Mansions, Tsim Sha Tsui. 2368 1689. www.venere.com.
One of the best-kept accommodations in the Chungking Mansions, Park Guest House is equipped with surveillance cameras. Tiny rooms all come with air-conditioning.

The Anne Black – YWCA
$$$ **169 rooms**
5 Man Fuk Rd., Waterloo Road Hill, Mong Kok. 2713 9211. hotel.ywca.org.hk.
Set up on a hillside, far from the bustle of the center of Mong Kok, this quiet establishment will be the joy of light sleepers, despite the slightly worn rooms. There is a women-only floor, and an additional charge for breakfast and Internet access.

HOTELS

Rent-A-Room

$$$ **70 rooms**

7-8 Tak Hing St., Apt A, 2nd floor, Knight Garden (behind the Pridention Shopping Center), Jordan, Tsim Sha Tsui. 2366 3011 or 3422 9229. rentaroomhk.com.

For tranquility in the heart of Tsim Sha Tsui, this guest house fits the bill. It is located in a residence set back off Nathan Road. Peace and quiet are luxuries that must be paid for, but local calls, tea, coffee and local newspapers come compliments of the house.

Hullet House

$$$$ **10 Suites**

2A Canton Rd., Tsim Sha Tsui. 3988 0000. www.hulletthouse.com.

This former Marine Police Headquarters offers 10 refined suites, though the building's conversion to a hotel and upscale boutiques draws mixed opinions from local residents. Themes of individually decorated rooms reflect their names. One four-poster bed is topped with a green and red roof inspired by a Confucian temple; day-glo Mao Zedong renditions on canvases adorn the walls of another.

Kowloon Shangri-La

$$$$ **688 rooms**

64 Mody Rd., Tsim Sha Tsui. 2721 2111. www.shangri-la.com.

On the edge of Victoria Harbour, right off the Tsim Sha Tsui promenade, Shangra-La affords a striking view of Hong Kong Island. From its marble-floored lobby to its elegantly appointed rooms, the hotel oozes traditional luxury. The property's restaurants offer a mix of cuisines including Japanese, Cantonese and Italian.

Langham Place

$$$$ **665 rooms**

555 Shanghai St., Mong Kok. 3552 3388. hongkong.langham placehotels.com.

This sumptuous high-tech hotel adjoins Langham Place mall. Flat-screen TVs; DVD/CD players and iHome docking stations are standard here, along with work stations boasting state-of-the-art telephones and wireless Internet access. Take time to luxuriate at Chuan Spa.

The Luxe Manor

$$$$ **159 rooms**

39 Kimberly Rd., Tsim Sha Tsui. 3763 8828. www.theluxe manor.com.

Billing itself as a "celebration of the abstract," The Luxe Manor is indeed quirky but elegant. The façade of the hotel, as its name implies, looks like a residential building. The hotel caters to business travelers with Wi-Fi throughout the property. Rooms sport playful surreal touches, and the six themed suites are decked out in exuberant design. Dada Bar hosts good live music.

The Mira

$$$$ **492 rooms**

118-130 Nathan Rd., Tsim Sha Tsui. 2368 1111. www.themira hotel com.

Formerly the Miramar, this hotel recently gained a renovation and lost a syllable to become the Mira. Now a sleek ambience and a pastry counter accent the lobby. Soothing color schemes and clean lines mark the rooms, which also feature gadgets aplenty: LCD flat-screen TVs, Bose sound systems and free Wi-Fi Internet access.

Check out the hotel's **Cuisine Cuisine** restaurant for superb Cantonese fare.

The Peninsula
$$$$ 500 rooms
Salisbury Rd., Tsim Sha Tsui. 2920 2888. www.peninsula.com.
Known as The Pen to regulars, this retro symbol of British Hong Kong is one of the city's paragons of luxury – as evidenced by the liveried grooms and the fleet of Rolls Royces lined up outside. Inside, marble baths, harbor panoramas (from the tower rooms) and an opulent Asian-accented Victorian style will wrap you in comfort. A colonnaded rooftop pool, on-site spa, and delicious dining options are just a few more reasons you'll want to stay here.

 Ritz-Carlton Hong Kong
$$$$ 312 rooms
ICC, 1 Austin Rd. West, West Kowloon. 3717 2222. www.ritzcarlton.com.
Opened in March 2011 at the pinnacle of Hong Kong's tallest tower, the International Commerce Centre, the Ritz delivers nothing short of ultimate luxury. Décor fit for a king vies with killer views across the territory for attention, while a neutral palette warms guestrooms that boast the likes of Blu-ray DVD players and A-list bathroom amenities. Perched on the 118th floor, **Ozone** restaurant and bar is the new place to see and be seen.

The Royal Garden
$$$$ 419 rooms
69 Mody Rd., Tsim Sha Tsui. 2721 5215. www.rghk.com.hk.
Overlooking Victoria Harbour, The Royal Garden arranges its rooms around a bright interior courtyard. The rooftop brims with well-being options; a Mediterranean-inspired swimming pool, heated in winter, is the highlight, along with tennis courts, and a gym and sauna. The hotel's **Dong Lai Shun** restaurant is famed for its *shaun yang rou*, thin slices of boiled Mongolian mutton.

W Hong Kong
$$$$ 393 rooms
1 Austin Rd. West, West Kowloon. 3717 2222. www.starwood hotels.com.

W Hong Kong

The W appeals to a younger set with its zen-like contemporary rooms and rooftop pool, the scene of popular cocktail parties in summer. A state-of-the-art entertainment system is de rigueur, as is a "Munchie Box" filled with surprises. Rooms are wired for Wi-Fi Internet. If you need anything else, the W's signature "Whatever/ Whenever" team is on duty 24/7– just push the designated button on your room phone.

HOTELS

Outlying Islands

Both weekday (less expensive) and weekend rates are indicated below.

B&B

$$-$$$ 18 rooms
Tung Wan Beach, Tung Wan Rd., Cheung Chau Island. 2986 9990. www.bbcheungchau.com.hk.
More a hotel than a B&B, this establishment in the village of Cheung Chau, has small but well-kept rooms. From the rooftop terrace you can watch the sun rise and set over the village.

Bali Hotel Resort

$$-$$$ 28 rooms
8 Main St., Yung Shue Wan, Lamma Island. 2982 4580. www.lammabali.com.
Some accommodations at the Bali have a kitchen, and all are equipped with a microwave and small refrigerator. Rooms facing the port have a small balcony, but noise from the pier on weekends can be distracting.

Man Lai Wah Hotel

$$-$$$ 9 rooms
2 Po Wah Garden, Yung Shue Wan, Lamma Island. 2982 0220.
If you're looking for budget accommodations with a harbor view, try this simple place. It's the first hotel you come to at the end of the ferry pier.

Mui Wo Inn

$$-$$$ 9 rooms
Silvermine Bay, Mui Wo, Lantau Island. 2984 7225.
At the end of the Silvermine Bay beach, this hotel is recognizable by its terrace, set about with kitschy Greek statues. Rooms were renovated in 2008; for a few more dollars, you can get one that looks out to sea.

Concerto Inn

$$$-$$$$ 14 rooms
28 Hung Shing Yeh Beach, Yung Shue Wan, Lamma Island. 2982 1668. www.concertoinn.com.hk.
This hotel on the beach, 25 minutes from the Yung Shue Wan ferry terminal, is probably the most stylish establishment on the island. The more expensive rooms face the sea, and eight newly renovated rooms enjoy Wi-Fi Internet access, DVD, iPOD dock, and a rain shower.

Warwick Hotel

$$$-$$$$ 63 rooms
East Bay, Cheung Chau Island. 2981 0081. www.warwickhotel. com.hk.
Bright, comfortable guestrooms here have balconies facing Cheung Chau's beach. Amenities include a swimming pool, a game room/library and a small spa. The staff can arrange for activities like windsurfing, sea kayaking and fishing trips.

Hong Kong Disneyland Hotel

$$$$ 400 rooms
Hong Kong Disneyland, Penny's Bay, Lantau Island. 3510 5000. www.hongkongdisneyland.com.
Can't get enough of Hong Kong Disneyland? Two on-site hotels include not only access to the park, but also character breakfasts with Mickey and his pals. Overlooking the sea, the sparkling white Disneyland Hotel is done in Victorian style. Next door, **Disneyland's Hollywood Hotel** (**$$$**) sports a spiffy Art Deco ambience.

MUST STAY

Macau

$ less than MOP150
$$ MOP150-300
$$$ MOP300-600
$$$$ MOP600-900
$$$$$ more than MOP900

 Hotel Ko Wah

$$ **5 rooms**
*71 Rua da Felicidade, Peninsula
Macau. 2893 0755.*

This lively street, where some
hotels occasionally accommodate
prostitutes and their clients, is
the meeting place for Macau's
backpackers. Clean and pleasant,
the modest Ko Wah is an exception
to this rule. The hotel represents
a good value at this location, a
few steps away from the most
happening parts of Macau.

 Poussada de Coloane

$$$ **30 rooms**
*Cheoc Van Beach, Colôane.
2888 2143. www.hotelpcoloane.
com.mo.*

This charming, if weathered, inn is
a haven of tranquility on a hillside
overlooking Cheoc Van Beach.
The staff is attentive and rooms
feature tiled walls, solid-wood
bed frames and, in the more
luxurious chambers, bathrooms
with Jacuzzis. Some even have
balconies with ocean views.
The poolside restaurant serves
excellent Portuguese cuisine.

The Galaxy

$$$$$ **2,200 rooms**
*Cotai Strip. 2888 0888.
www.galaxymacau.com.*

New hospitality kid on the
block, palatial Galaxy Macau
incorporates three top-tier hotels,
plus restaurants and gaming areas
within its complex. On the grounds
of the resort, there are also 250
suites and villas at the **Banyan
Tree Macau**, and 500 rooms and
suites at the **Hotel Okura Macau**.

The Venetian Macao

$$$$$ **3,000 rooms**
*Estrada da Baía de Nossa Senhora
da Esperança, Taipa. 2882 8888.
www.venetianmacao.com.*

Gondolas in Macau? You'll
find them at this casino hotel,
which expresses the height of
excess. The largest casino in the
world, Venetian Macao offers
lavish and spacious all-suite
accommodations. Some 800
gaming tables attract high-rollers
from Mainland China and beyond.

The Venetian Macao

© Elwynn/Dreamstime.com

 Wynn Macau

$$$$$ **1,014 rooms**
*Rua Cidade de Sintra,
Nape District. 8986 9966.
www.wynnmacau.com.*

The Vegas glam factor appears
everywhere you look in this
casino hotel. Opulence is key in
materials throughout; rooms are
sumptuous with a modern edge.
When you need a break, check out
the Wynn's spa, chic shops, the
jellyfish aquarium or the splendid
outdoor pool.

HOTELS

HONG KONG

INDEX

INDEX

159

 NOTES